JESUS AND THE PHARISEES

JESUS AND THE PHARISEES

JOHN BOWKER
LECTURER IN DIVINITY, UNIVERSITY OF CAMBRIDGE, AND
FELLOW OF CORPUS CHRISTI COLLEGE

CAMBRIDGE
AT THE UNIVERSITY PRESS
1973

CAMBRIDGE UNIVERSITY PRESS
Cambridge, New York, Melbourne, Madrid, Cape Town, Singapore, São Paulo, Delhi

Cambridge University Press
The Edinburgh Building, Cambridge CB2 8RU, UK

Published in the United States of America by Cambridge University Press, New York

www.cambridge.org
Information on this title: www.cambridge.org/9780521200554

First published 1973
This digitally printed version 2008

A catalogue record for this publication is available from the British Library

Library of Congress Catalogue Card Number: 72–87439

ISBN 978-0-521-20055-4 hardback
ISBN 978-0-521-09732-1 paperback

CONTENTS

For Margaret

שלי שלך

PREFACE

This book has been written to serve as a companion to studies of the Pharisees, and in particular to discussions of the Pharisees as they occur in the New Testament. It consists of an Introduction, an additional note on the controversies between the Pharisees (and others) and the Sadducees, and a translation of original source material bearing on the discussions.

The main part of the book consists of the translations, from both Greek and Semitic sources (though not from Bible or apocrypha which are more easily available). Obviously, not *all* the passages of possible relevance could be included, since that would have required at least another volume; but an attempt has been made to include the passages which are indispensable for an understanding of the Pharisees, and which occur frequently in discussion. It must, however, be borne in mind that the passages necessarily occur out of context, and may require the context for their full understanding.

The translations have been grouped in nine separate sections (see the list of Contents). Throughout the book, references without further specification of a particular work are to the translations, by section and number within the section (for example, 1.1, 1.2, 1.3, etc. refer to the section of translations from Josephus).

The book is deliberately intended to be introductory: to understand the Pharisees is not easy, and the purpose of this book is to offer some initial bearings in very difficult country. For this reason, the Introduction has been kept as direct and simple as possible: it represents the structure of a possible argument, rather than the full argument itself, since almost every point in it could be given much more detailed elaboration, and no doubt much more cautious qualification as well. But that kind of elaboration would probably prove confusing to those who are not already familiar with the field. As it is, the Introduction outlines a solution to the difficult problem of identifying the 'Pharisees' in the different sources, and it suggests a new approach to the understanding of Jesus in relation to the Pharisees (particularly as recorded in Mark), and to his 'trial'. Even if these suggestions seem unconvincing, the Introduction may nevertheless still help to make clear what the problems are. I hope, at the very least, that New Testament discussions will cease to talk (as some undoubtedly have) of the Pharisees as though they were an undifferentiated group without a history of their own.

The Introduction presupposes at least some knowledge of the history of the period in question, even if only in narrative or outline form. It also presupposes my earlier book, *The Targums and Rabbinic Literature*, Cambridge, 1969, the Introduction of which was equally intended to offer some initial bearings in the field of rabbinic biblical exegesis, together with the briefest possible description of rabbinic works and references.

So far as possible (and where they exist) existing translations have been used, but they have been corrected where necessary, particularly in the interests of uniformity. For the Bible, the translation is that of the New English Bible, for Josephus it is that of the Loeb translation, for the Mishnah, it is that of H. Danby (since this is the most widely used; but note the translation of P. Blackman which frequently corrects it), and for the Babylonian Talmud, it is that of the Soncino translation.

My thanks are offered to Dr Knopf and Dr de Langhe, who looked at parts of the translation and suggested corrections and improvements. They are not, of course, responsible for the mistakes that undoubtedly remain. Translations can, at best, serve as indications of possible meaning, but in the end there is no substitute for the text itself. Nevertheless, I hope that these translations will make the discussion of the Pharisees, and of the relation of Jesus to his contemporaries, easier for those who find the original texts difficult, either to find, or to understand. But ultimately, reference to the texts is indispensable.

My thanks are also offered to Miss J. M. Gurley, who typed what was often a complicated manuscript; and above all, to Margaret, my wife, who encouraged me to persist with this book in circumstances which made it seem likely that the writing of it would not be possible. Whatever its shortcomings, I hope it may at least be of some service to others.

June 1972 J.W.B.

ABBREVIATIONS

Ant. *Antiquities*
A.R.N. Aboth deRabbi Nathan
Ass. Mos. Assumption of Moses
A.Z. Abodah Zarah
B. Babli
B.B. Baba Bathra
Baḥod. Baḥodesh
Bek. Bekoroth
Bem.R. Bemidbar Rabbah
B.Q. Baba Qamma
Ber. Berakoth
B.Z. *Biblische Zeitschrift*
C.D.C. The Damascus Rule
Dem. Demai
De Prov. *De Providentia*
De Spec. Leg. *De Specialibus Legibus*
Eduy. Eduyyoth
Erub. Erubin
Gitt. Gittin
Ḥag. Ḥagigah
Hor. Horayoth
H.S.S. *Harvard Semitic Series*
H.T.R. *Harvard Theological Review*
H.U.C.A. *Hebrew Union College Annual*
Ḥull. Ḥullin
J. Jerushalmi
J.B.L. *Journal of Biblical Literature*
J.Q.R. *Jewish Quarterly Review*
Kasp. Kaspa
Kel. Kelim
Ket. Ketuboth
M. Mishnah
Makk. Makkoth
Maksh. Makshirin
Meg. Ta'an. Megillath Ta'anith
Men. Menaḥoth
M.Sh. Ma'aser Sheni
Nidd. Niddah
N.T.S. *New Testament Studies*
Par. Parah
Pes. Pesaḥim
Pes.R. Pesiqta Rabbati
Proc.I.A.S.H. *Proceedings of the Israel Academy of Sciences and Humanities*
Qid. Qiddushin
Qoh.R. Qoheleth Rabbah
R.H. Rosh haShanah
Rn. Rabban
San. Sanhedrin
Shab. Shabbath
Sheb. Shebi'ith
Sheq. Sheqalim
Sot. Sotah
Sukk. Sukkah
T. Tosefta
Tanḥ.B. Tanḥuma (Buber's edn.)
Toh. Tohoroth
Vay.R. Vayyiqra Rabbah
Yad. Yadaim
Yeb. Yebamoth
Yom. Yoma
Zeb. Zebaḥim
Z.N.T.W. *Zeitschrift für die neutestamentliche Wissenschaft*

ACKNOWLEDGEMENTS

Acknowledgement is due to the Clarendon Press, Oxford, for permission to quote from the Mishnah, translated by Herbert Danby; the Loeb Classical Library and Harvard University Press, for permission to quote from their translation of Josephus; and to the Soncino Press, for permission to quote the Soncino translation of the Babylonian Talmud, under the general editorship of Rabbi Dr I. Epstein, with the following translators for the passages involved: I. Abrahams, A. Cohen, S. Daiches, H. Freedman, L. Jung, H. M. Lazarus, L. Miller, A. Mishcon, J. Schachter, M. Simon, I. W. Slotki.

NOTE ON TRANSLITERATIONS

No attempt has been made to achieve consistency in the transliteration of Semitic words. In the Introduction, transliterations have been given in full (i.e. with vowels supplied), in order to assist those without a knowledge of Semitic languages to read the text in a straightforward way. In the Translations, the transliteration is mainly consonantal, but not in the case of words or phrases which have become standard (e.g. *dibre sopherim*, *'am haAreẓ*); but in the case of the Dead Sea Scrolls, the vocalisation has been given, because this indicates the reading adopted as a basis for the translation. *Perushim* becomes, in the Translations, *prushim* to serve as a reminder that each occurrence of the term has to be separately evaluated, and not taken to mean 'Pharisees' without further reflection.

INTRODUCTION

The problems of identifying the Pharisees

There are two reasons why it is now virtually (perhaps totally) impossible to write an adequate history of the Pharisees: the first is that there is far too little evidence; and the second, that there is far too much. On the one hand, surprisingly little direct information about the Pharisees has survived: from this point of view alone, a detailed account of the Pharisees is not possible.[1] Yet on the other hand, a number of sources do in fact refer to a group or sect known, in English transliteration, as the Pharisees – and for many people, the most familiar of the references are those in the Gospels. But since the Pharisees appear, in both Christian and Jewish sources, as a part of a very complex history, it follows that the Pharisees cannot be studied in isolation, but only as a part of the history of the whole Jewish people in the period in question – principally, the period of the so-called second commonwealth (from the restoration after the Exile to the fall of Jerusalem in 70 C.E.), and of the following hundred years. Furthermore, it is clear that in some sense the Pharisees were related to rabbinic Judaism as its predecessors, and from *this* point of view, a knowledge of the formation of rabbinic Judaism is necessary for any serious understanding of the Pharisees; and it is here that the problem of too much evidence becomes formidable, since rabbinic sources are extensive, and are not always easy to understand. But even a brief acquaintance with the rabbinic sources makes it clear that the sense in which the Pharisees were the predecessors of the rabbis is by no means simple or direct. Nothing could be more misleading than to refer to the Pharisees without further qualification as the predecessors of the rabbis, for the fact remains that 'Pharisees' are attacked in rabbinic sources as vigorously as 'Pharisees' are attacked in the Gospels, and often for similar reasons. There is thus an initial problem in identifying the

[1] So, e.g., E. Rivkin, 'Pharisaism and the Crisis of the Individual in the Greco-Roman World', *J.Q.R.* LXI, 1970, 27–53: 'The history of Pharisaism is largely non-recoverable because of the nature of the sources' (p. 31, n. 4).

references to 'Pharisees' in the different sources, and in determining whether, in fact, they refer to the same group or groups.

The initial problem can be stated quite simply. The Greek language sources (particularly Josephus and the N.T.) refer to a group known as *pharisaioi*, the Semitic language sources (particularly the rabbinic sources) refer to identifiable groups of people known as *perushim*. Both *pharisaioi* and *perushim* can legitimately, though loosely, be transliterated as 'Pharisees'. But the accounts given of the *pharisaioi* in Josephus and of the *perushim* in the rabbinic sources differ so much that the question has frequently been raised whether the terms *pharisaioi* and *perushim* refer to the same group, or whether *perushim* refers to a group, or party, at all.

Josephus gave surprisingly little information about the Pharisaioi, considering that he had, according to his own account, governed his life by the rule of the Pharisaioi, at least for some time (1.22). There are three general descriptions of the Pharisaioi (1.1, 1.12 (12ff.), 1.18 (162f.)), but no detailed account of their organisation or method, nor is their name explained; nor, for that matter, is there any account of when or how the Pharisaioi emerged: the reference in 1.1 is imprecise, though the 'time' referred to is, in the context, *c.* 144 B.C.E., since Josephus inserted the reference after his account of Jonathan's negotiations with Rome and Sparta (I Macc. xii.1–23). Apart from the general descriptions, Josephus' portrayal of the Pharisaioi is incidental; and in the incidents described they emerge as a coherent group, able to remain in being even when excluded by the prevailing authorities from direct participation in government (as, for example, by John Hyrcanus (1.2), or by Alexander Jannaeus (1.3 and 1.4)). At times, nevertheless, they were in favour, as under Salome Alexandra (1.4, and the further references), and they were in any case able to make their voice heard, either because of their ability (1.6 (172, 176); 1.12 (15); 1.19 (411); 1.20 (159)) or because of their influence with the people (1.2 (288, 298); 1.4 (401); 1.12 (15)). It is clear from Josephus that a fundamental and differentiating characteristic was their adherence to the Law together with a procedure of traditional interpretation which established a relation between the Law as originally given and the customary application of it by the people. Josephus frequently emphasised the sacrosant nature of the Law, to which nothing should be added or removed (1.21; cf. also 1.13), and he regarded innovation as a major cause of the revolt against Rome (e.g., 1.12 (9); 1.19 (414)). The genius of the Pharisaioi lay in their ability to hold together customary tradition and the given Law; whereas it is clear that Josephus regarded the Sadducees as introducing a conflict between the literal Law as given and the customary interpretation which had arisen through succeeding generations.

There would be little point summarising, in this essay, what Josephus wrote about the Pharisaioi, since the material is included in the Translations. However, since the excerpts follow the order in which they appear in Josephus, it may be helpful to offer a more schematic guide for those who wish to read the material as a whole:

General descriptions of Jewish groups, including the Pharisaioi:

1.1; 1.12; 1.18; see also 1.2 (297f.)

Incidents, in chronological order:

a. the break with John Hyrcanus: 1.2

b. the break with Alexander Jannaeus: 1.3

c. the restoration under Salome: 1.4; 1.14

d. (a reference to the appointment of Hyrcanus: 1.5)

e. the opposition of Samaias/Pollion to Herod when young: 1.6 (172ff.); cf. 1.15

f. Samaias and Pollion favoured by Herod: 1.7

g. Herod's oath of loyalty refused by the Pharisaioi: 1.9

h. their influence with Pheroras' wife and the women of the court: 1.10; 1.16

i. the cutting down of the golden eagle above the Temple gate: 1.11; 1.17

j. Saddok the Pharisee assists the opposition to Quirinius: 1.12; cf. 1.18

k. their counsel at the approach of the revolt against Rome: 1.19

l. the counsel of Gorion b. Joseph and Simeon b. Gamaliel (cf. 1.24 (191)): 1.20

m. Josephus consults the *protoi Pharisaioi* during the Revolt: 1.23

n. Pharisaioi are among those who investigate Josephus during the Revolt: 1.24

Additional passages which illustrate other points:

1.13; 1.14: the high estimate of the Law in Josephus

1.22: his own association with the Pharisaioi

1.8: a passage to which reference is sometimes made as a possible explanation of the origin of the Boethusians

1.5: an illustration of the use of *synhedria* as a general term

The account of the Pharisaioi in Josephus will be seen, from this material, to be reasonably consistent. Allowances no doubt have to be made for Josephus' partiality, and for his purposes in writing Jewish histories at all, but the fact remains that there is nothing absurdly implausible in his account, brief and incidental as it is. But when one turns to the Semitic sources, in relation to Josephus, the problems of interpretation become very great. The basic problem can be stated, once more, quite simply: those whom Josephus referred to as Pharisaioi are to some extent linked with, or related to, those whom the later rabbis regarded as their own legitimate predecessors. But the rabbis scarcely ever referred to their predecessors as *perushim* (a possible, though interpretative, Semitic way of expressing the Greek *pharisaioi*); they referred to them by many names, but particularly, in their role as transmitters and interpreters of Torah, as Ḥakamim (the Wise, or the Sages). Almost without exception, they do not refer to their predecessors as *perushim*; on the contrary (as has already been observed), the rabbinic sources contain attacks directed *against perushim* – attacks which are almost as violent as the attacks on the Pharisaioi in the Gospels. What, if any, is the connection between the Pharisaioi of Josephus and the *perushim* of the rabbinic sources?

An obvious answer is to say that there is no connection at all. The root *prsh* can convey a meaning of 'separation', and there are certainly instances of this in the rabbinic sources (as illustrated on pp. 6f., 14). On this argument, the word *perushim* (or in the singular *parush*) is a way of referring to those who separate themselves in some way – either, for example, in extreme holiness, or in schism from the main community. The word *perushim* cannot, on this view be taken to mean 'Pharisees' as such. Since it is used to describe 'separatists', it *may* on occasion refer to those whom Josephus described as Pharisaioi, but there should be no expectation that this will be the case in every instance of the word *perushim*. Indeed, the word may not necessarily refer to an organised party or group at all, but simply to those who in some way separate themselves. The uses of *parush* and *perushim* must be tested on each occasion to determine their reference; they cannot, without further question, be assumed to supply information about the Pharisaioi.[1]

There is much strength in this argument, not least because, as has been stated already, the later rabbis did not refer to their own predecessors as *perushim*; among many different names, principally Ḥakamim, the name *perushim* scarcely ever occurs. Furthermore, there is no real doubt that the Pharisaioi of Josephus are related to the Ḥakamim. In addition to the general descriptions of Josephus, which are reasonably consistent with what is known of the Ḥakamim, particular incidents correlate in Josephus and in the rabbinic sources. Here, of course, it must be borne in mind that specific historical reference, for its own sake, is extremely rare in most rabbinic works, and that details are often brief and imprecise. Even when incidents are referred to in rabbinic works which can also be

[1] See the further, and highly important, article by Rivkin, 'Defining the Pharisees: the Tannaitic Sources', *H.U.C.A.* XL, 1969, 205–49. In this article, an attempt is made to establish a methodology for defining the Pharisees in the Tannaitic sources. Rivkin suggested two controls: first, the passages which refer to Pharisees (*prushim*) collectively in juxtaposition and opposition to the Sadducees; these 'should be collated and the definition that they yield extracted' (p. 208). Second, the passages 'where the term *prushim* is conceded by scholars to mean something other than Pharisees' (p. 208); these also should be collated. The passages mentioning *prushim* which do not fall into the two control categories should then be examined without reference to the controls to see what information they reveal. This should then be compared with the control passages to see where identity or distinction obtains. The first control definition of the Pharisees can thus be extended, and the more usual way of defining the Pharisees from Josephus and the N.T. (often without much reference to the rabbinic sources) can itself be controlled and checked. The method proposed by Rivkin clearly cannot be absolute, because it cannot eliminate the need for ordinary historical judgement in those cases where identity or distinction is insufficiently precise, nor can it establish *in itself* that group uses of *prushim* refer to the same group. But its importance lies in its attempt to discriminate among different uses of *prushim*. The same general point of view, that discrimination is needed, is followed in this Introduction.

found in Josephus, the main interest of the rabbinic recorder is likely to have been explanatory or exemplary; that is to say, his purpose is likely to have been to explain or exemplify a particular interpretation of Torah, or to illustrate when it originated, or how it came about. For this reason, stories occur in different places in rabbinic works with the names of participants changed or inverted, or with circumstantial details altered. But the critical point is that the substance, or purpose, of the narrative may well persist unchanged, even though the circumstantial details, or the names, are insecure. This does not mean that the substance of a narrative can automatically be assumed to go back to the original moment; it *does* mean that once a narrative emerged to exemplify a particular point, or points, it is likely to have persisted for as long as those points needed exemplifying in that particular way – which may, in fact, be down to the present day. Obviously, it is rash to generalise; but it is equally rash to assume that if a conflict of detail exists between Josephus and a rabbinic source, the rabbinic source is *wholly* to be discounted (or, for that matter, that Josephus is wholly to be discounted). Yet even with these necessary reservations in mind, it is sufficiently clear that the Pharisaioi in Josephus do, at least to some extent, overlap with the Ḥakamim.

In view of the relation between the Ḥakamim and the Pharisaioi, and of the fact that the later rabbis did not, in general, refer to their predecessors as *perushim*, there is an obvious strength in the argument that *perushim* are not to be confused or identified with the Pharisaioi. If the Pharisaioi are to be cross-identified, it should be with the Ḥakamim, and even then cautiously: there is no guarantee of the absolute accuracy of Josephus' use of Pharisaioi at every point. So on this argument, the term *perushim* does not refer to the Pharisaioi of Josephus, but to various individuals or groups who separated themselves in some manner. If the argument is examined, the first and most obvious point in its favour is the fact that there is not the slightest doubt that the root *prsh* carries, in many instances, a meaning of separation. A basic example occurs in 6.7; in 4.23 it refers to the separation of tithe; and in 5.4 to a separation of people. It is frequently used to describe separation from a community – not necessarily Israel: in 2.34 and 3.17 it refers to separation from the Samaritans; in 6.6 from the daughters of Israel. A particularly good example of this usage occurs in 4.10, since here both the verb and the noun (*perushim*) are used; and it is quite clear that the word *perushim* is used by a rabbi of those who detached themselves from the Ḥakamim, not of the predecessors of the rabbis! The contrast between Ḥakamim and *perushim* is clear, even though R. Ashi was commenting at a later time.

A distinction between the Ḥakamim and the *perushim* is also suggested by the passage (2.38) in which Rn. Joḥanan b. Zakkai, one of the greatest figures in the Ḥakamic/rabbinic tradition, speaks of the *perushim* as though separate from himself. But here it has to be noted that he argues *for* the *perushim* against the Sadducees. There is thus a measure of distinction, but a measure of association as well. It is uncertain how accurate the passage is in detail, since Joḥanan b. Zakkai appears frequently as the protagonist against the Sadducees (and with great formal similarity in some instances). It thus appears to have been almost a 'literary genre' to cast Joḥanan in this role;[1] so although the disputes are *prima facie* likely to have occurred in substance, the detailed presentation appears to have become increasingly standardised. Nevertheless, the fact remains that Joḥanan's reference to the *perushim* as though distinct from himself is *not* a standard part of the usual presentation, and there is no real reason to doubt it.

Another similar example of distinction and yet of association between Ḥakamim and *perushim* can be found in 4.37. It will be pointed out below that the Sadducees, although in control of the Temple, had in many instances to follow the rulings or the interpretations of the Ḥakamim, exactly as Josephus stated (1.12 (17)), and as the rabbinic sources frequently exemplify (e.g. 2.11; 2.12; 2.32).[2] The version of the anecdote in the Tosefta (3.17 (3)) mentions only the Ḥakam; in the Babylonian Talmud, the *perushim* are mentioned as though distinct from the Ḥakamim, and yet clearly in close association with them.

Even more dramatic than these examples are the instances in which *perushim* are strongly attacked in the rabbinic sources – condemnations which were scarcely likely to have been made if the *perushim* were regarded as the predecessors of the rabbis – i.e. as the Pharisaioi of Josephus. For example, in the Mishnah (2.21) an unelaborated reference is made to *makkot perushim*, the wounds, or blows, of the *perushim*. The *gemara* in the Babylonian Talmud (4.22)

[1] For references to Joḥanan b. Zakkai, see the Index.

[2] But note, e.g., 2.8, 2.23, which exemplify that the priests did not always conform.

gives its own interpretation of the meaning of the phrase by defining seven types of *perushim*. Some of the definitions are obscure but it is clear in general that they were intended to be condemnatory, since otherwise the comment at one point, 'But that is a virtue!' would make no sense. In 5.14, the phrase *makkot perushim* is defined by two stories as deception. The condemnation of *perushim* is equally clear in the discussion of the meaning of *minim* in the Shemoneh 'Esreh (the Eighteen Benedictions). The meanings of the word *minim* are by no means certain, but at least it can be said that the word refers to opponents of those whom the rabbis regarded as legitimately Jewish – hence the curse on them in the Shemoneh 'Esreh. According to the Palestinian Talmud (5.2), the wicked are associated with the *minim*; but in the parallel discussion in Tosefta (3.1), it is the *perushim* who are associated with the *minim*; there is thus an association between the *minim*, the *perushim* and the 'wicked'.

Thus far it would seem that the case for dissociating *perushim* from Pharisaioi is strong, since the rabbis, in the examples given, dissociated *themselves* from the *perushim*, sometimes in strongly condemnatory terms. But the issue is not quite so simple, for in fact, there are a few instances where a connection between Ḥakamim and *perushim* exists, just as, in some of the examples above, a measure of association could be discerned as well as of dissociation. The basic example is 4.25, the account in the Babylonian Talmud of what is also described in Josephus as a breach between Hyrcanus and the Pharisaioi (1.2). There are obvious conflicts between the two accounts, not least the name of the king – though the name Jannai may simply be a consequence of abbreviation through the letter *yodh*, at a later stage in transmission. But however imprecise the rabbinic memory of the episode may be, the fact remains that *perushim* and Ḥakamim are associated as a single group in the first incident (chronologically) in which, in Josephus, the name Pharisaioi is used. What must be observed is that it is the *opponent* of the Ḥakamim who uses the term *perushim* to describe them. This is exactly the case in a second fundamentally important example, the account in A.R.N. (6.1) of the origin of the Sadducees and Boethusians.

The context of this passage requires a slightly longer discussion. The holding of the high priesthood and the legitimacy of the high priest were constant and fundamental issues among Jews during the period from the Maccabean revolt to the destruction of the Temple –

as, indeed, they were among the issues which precipitated the Maccabean revolt itself, since the attempt to make the high priesthood a matter of barter inevitably antagonised those who stressed the purity of Zadokite descent. At one point, shortly before the Revolt, there were five claimants to the high priesthood, and the extreme Zadokites went so far in their opposition to what was happening to the high priesthood in the Temple at Jerusalem that they withdrew to Leontopolis and built their own Temple there – no doubt waiting for the restoration of their own pure line of descent in better days. Those who remained in Jerusalem did not necessarily agree with the arrangements in the Temple, but they were prepared to accept them. When the Hasmonaean family became successful rulers, it was virtually inevitable that they would take over the vitally important office of high priest, even though they were in the strictest sense unqualified: in the post-exilic period the high priest had become the leader of the Jewish community, and the Hasmonaeans could scarcely be leaders of that community in any full sense without becoming high priests. But it was obviously necessary to find some way of allowing them to be high priests despite their ostensible lack of full qualification. I Macc. xiv records the settlement reached with reference to Simon, and it is clear that although Simon was recognised as high priest, it was with reservation. Emphasis is placed on the political aspects of his leadership, but apart from a general reference to his full charge of the Temple (vs. 42), little or no reference is made to specifically religious duties. Furthermore, the compromise nature of the arrangements is clearly recognised in the phrase 'until a true prophet should appear' (vs. 41): Simon and his successors were accepted as high priests but only until the unusual circumstances could be rectified by the consummation of the covenant promises of God, and by the restoration of his direct guidance to the community. It is thus clear that although Simon and his successors were recognised as high priests, it was only on the condition that certain specifically religious matters were reserved away from them, in view of their lack of qualification.

The high priesthood was thus a divisive issue in this period,[1] and

[1] It is thus important to note that the cause of division between Hyrcanus and the Pharisaioi/Ḥakamim was, according to both Josephus and the rabbinic tradition (1.2, 4.25), the technical disqualification of Hyrcanus in his claim to be high priest. Other, and quite different examples, of strong feelings about the high priesthood will be found in 1.20 and 4.9. Note also the (probably) anti-Hasmonaean passage in 9.1.

indeed throughout the period it was divided among different families, of varying degrees of qualification. The rabbis recognised two main groups among the Temple priests (at least in the later part of the period), the Sadducees and the Boethusians,[1] though they knew that other families were involved as well. They also recognised that although some individual priests were members of the Ḥakamic movement,[2] and although the Temple priests (including the high priest) were in many instances compelled to implement Ḥakamic interpretations in the Temple (particularly where the interpretations defended traditional procedures),[3] the fact remained that in general the Sadducees and the Boethusians opposed the Ḥakamim and resisted their influence. Various controversies between them have been recorded;[4] they are of great importance in understanding the history of the period, and particularly in understanding the content of the N.T., since they pre-date the fall of Jerusalem: after that date, the Sadducees effectively began to disappear, and after the destruction of the Temple were no longer able to continue their position. Their literal adherence to the text of Scripture was revived by the Karaites, and some of the controversies were also revived, in rabbinic Judaism, in order to refute the Karaites; the Karaites were even referred to in controversy as Sadducees (as probably in Megillath Ta'anith), but all this was centuries later.[5] Although the controversies are recorded by the victors (the Ḥakamim/rabbis), and although the details may therefore have become imprecise, the controversies in substance are important, because they are unlikely to have been wholly invented in the rabbinic period, and they can therefore throw much light on the Ḥakamim, and on other Jewish groups.

In view of the fluctuating conflicts in this period over the high priesthood, it is not surprising that the exact origins of the two main priestly groups, the Sadducees and the Boethusians, are obscure. A possible, but highly speculative, explanation of their origin focuses

[1] Although the two 'houses' were recognised, the distinction between them was not always kept clear, as can be seen in the fact that the names are sometimes used interchangeably in different accounts of the same incident. See, e.g., 3.4, 4.12, 5.8. Equally, it is vital to bear in mind that the term 'Boethusians' does not necessarily refer to one single, identifiable, group: it may have diverse reference.

[2] See, for example, Aboth ii.8, Eduy. viii.2, Ḥag. ii.7 (2.18), Josephus *Life* 197 (1.24).

[3] See pp. 3, 12, 30f.

[4] See the Additional Note, p. 53.

[5] The term 'Sadducee' becomes in fact very diverse in rabbinic literature.

on the action of Herod as described in 1.8. It is suggested that when Pompey entered Jerusalem, at least some of the Egyptian Zadokites (i.e. those based on the Temple at Leontopolis)[1] saw an opportunity of ending the Hasmonaean line of 'high priests', and of re-establishing the pure Zadokite line in Jerusalem. But when they returned to Jerusalem, they did not in fact succeed in taking over the Temple. The reference to Simon b. Boethus as an Alexandrian suggests that this may have been his background; if so, the move of Herod, quite apart from securing him the object of his desire, was subtle, because it counterbalanced in Jerusalem two branches of Zadokites: those who had stayed in Jerusalem throughout the period of the Hasmonaeans, and those who claimed an uncontaminated line of descent. In any case, Herod's move weakened the power of the high priesthood (potentially rival to himself) by perpetuating division. If this argument is correct, the Sadducees represent the Jerusalem line of Zadokite descent, the Boethusians the Egyptian line of descent.[2]

[1] See p. 9.

[2] The argument has, in fact, been taken further (see, e.g., G. R. Driver, *The Judaean Scrolls*, Oxford, 1965, pp. 226–37) in order to explain the Zadokite connections of the Dead Sea Scrolls. On this argument, the 'purist' Zadokites became as dissatisfied with the Herodian situation as they had been with the pre-Hasmonaean and the Hasmonaean. When Herod interfered with the appointment of a high priest (1.8), a situation comparable to that which had compelled them to withdraw to Leontopolis in the first place appeared to have come into being. Some could perhaps accept the Herodian situation because he had at least appointed a legitimate person, but others objected to a quite different principle, the right of a ruler to appoint a high priest at all. It is these 'extreme extremists' who again detached themselves, this time to the Dead Sea, to join (not to found) an already existing 'protestant' group. This would explain the Zadokite emphasis in some of the sectarian documents, and it would also explain why some of the rebels fled to the Zadokite temple in Egypt at the end of the Jewish revolt, and why the Roman armies moved on to destroy it. As Driver put it: 'That some links are missing in the chain of argument here put forward is readily admitted; and these in the present rate (*sic*) of knowledge cannot and perhaps never will be made good. It does, however, provide an answer, however hypothetical, to several questions which have never been answered' (*op. cit.* p. 237). What certainly seems to be the case is that the sect of the sectarian documents was eclectic; that is to say, it attracted those who resented, in extreme terms, what was happening in Jerusalem and in the Temple, and who had in some cases actually been driven out. But they brought with them something of their previous beliefs and practices. It is thus probable that the community attracted

There is, of course, no hint of this in A.R.N. (6.1), although it is stated that the names come from two different family names. A.R.N. concentrates on the breach between the Sadducees and the Boethusians on the one side, and the Ḥakamic disciples on the other. The issue is one of those mentioned by Josephus as an issue between the Pharisaioi and the Sadducees, the resurrection and reward of the dead.[1] The root *prsh* is used in both directions: the Sadducees and the Boethusians are separatist in exactly the same way that Judah b. Durtai was separatist (4.10); but conversely, the Sadducees, in their rejection of the Ḥakamic belief that there will be rewards in heaven, call their opponents *perushim*. Here, once again, there is an association between Ḥakamim and *perushim*, and again the term is in the mouth of opponents.

Ḥakamim and *perushim* appear to be associated in another group of passages, 2.11, 3.4, 4.12, 5.8, which describe one of the controversies between Sadducees/Boethusians and Ḥakamim. The particular issue concerns the lighting of incense on the Day of Atonement, and it is in fact a good example of the way in which the priests were compelled to follow the Ḥakamic interpretation of Torah, even though they themselves disagreed with it. The passages referred to describe a formal recognition of the breach between them: 'He turned aside (√*prsh*) and wept, and they turned aside (√*prsh*) and wept.' 4.12 and 5.8 explain why this was done, and both record a story in which a particular high priest performed the ritual according to the Sadducaic/Boethusian interpretation. Accord-

some who had been in the Ḥakamic movement. This would explain why it is possible to discern certain points of contact with Ḥakamic beliefs (or with beliefs that the Ḥakamim would not have disputed), and yet why there is a clear distinction on particular issues, and perhaps even an attack, through a play on words, on the Ḥakamim as those who establish *ḥalaqoth*/*Halakoth* (8.9; cf. also 8.2). It is of interest that the root *prsh* is, in the sectarian documents, largely 'innocent': it is primarily used of interpretation, and a quite different root (*bdl*) is preferred for separation, particularly with the connotation of holiness (see the passages in Section 8 of the translations, and especially 8.5; see also 'The Verb "to separate" in the Damascus Document', in N. Wieder, *The Judaean Scrolls and Karaism*, London, 1962, pp. 161ff.). It is almost as though the Scrolls represent a transition stage, in which the claim to interpretation is being challenged and taken over, but no offensive connotation of *prsh* is allowed in its place because of the acceptance in the sect of the basic principle of separation; indeed, the sect obviously emphasised it even further. For a summary, see Driver, *op. cit.* pp. 80ff.

[1] See also 2.1 and 6.15.

ing to the Palestinian Talmud (5.8), the father of the priest in question rebuked him by saying that although the Boethusians have their own interpretation, they nevertheless act according to the precepts of the Ḥakamim. But in the Babylonian version the rebuke is differently phrased: 'Although we are Sadducees, we are afraid of the *perushim*.' Once again, it is an issue between the Sadducees/Boethusians and the Ḥakamim which elicits the term *perushim*, and again the term is put in the mouth of an opponent as his way of referring to the Ḥakamim. Furthermore, it seems likely that the story in 4.12 was in fact intended to be explanatory of the term *perushim* in relation to the Ḥakamim. A similar association of Ḥakamim and *perushim* can be seen in the dispute about inheritance: in 3.19 the *perushim* argue against the Sadducees: in 4.27 it is Joḥanan b. Zakkai. It is possible that the taunt of the Sadducees in 3.9 and 5.12 is another instance in which the Sadducees term as *perushim* those who implement a particular Ḥakamic interpretation in the Temple.

It follows that although there are undoubtedly condemnatory uses of *perushim*, it is possible to discern a recognition in rabbinic sources that there was a measure of association between *perushim* and Ḥakamim, and that *perushim* was a name applied to the Ḥakamim, at least by their opponents. Why was it abandoned, and how did it come about that *perushim* are so vigorously attacked in the rabbinic passages already referred to? The obvious answer is to say that *if perushim* was a term used by opponents of the Ḥakamim, the successors of the Ḥakamim were hardly likely to accept it as an appropriate name for themselves or for their predecessors, particularly if it meant 'separatist' (since they regarded themselves as the continuity of Israel, not as a sect). Although there is an element of truth in this, as will be seen, the whole answer is certainly not as simple as this, particularly since it leaves unexplained why the name Pharisaioi appears in Josephus without any apparent embarrassment, and certainly without offensive intention. The main reason why the answer cannot be so simple lies in the fact that the uses of *perushim* in the rabbinic sources are more varied than has emerged in the discussion so far. In particular, by no means all the uses of *perushim* are condemnatory: some passages stress the importance of separation in defining – and achieving – the command of God to his people to be holy, and they use the root *prsh* to do so.

Of particular importance in this respect are the group of Tannaitic passages, 6.4, 6.9, 6.12, 6.13, 6.14. In these, the necessary association of 'holiness' and 'separation' is clear:[1] if the fundamental command of God to his people to be holy – the command which in a sense constitutes his people – is to be fulfilled, it requires separation from anything unclean or from anything which might contaminate. But how can that separation be achieved? What does it *mean* to be holy? Torah is itself an answer to those questions, as also are the many interpretations of Torah in the long unfolding of the Ḥakamic/rabbinic tradition. In this sense, all Jews must be *perushim* in order to be Jews – in order, that is, to obey the command of God to be holy; and the remarkable thing is not that there are *good* senses of *perushim*, but that there are *bad* senses to be found, since in fact the notion of separation is indispensable to the notion of holiness.

The connection of separation and holiness in the root *prsh* is clear in many other passages. In the form *perishut*, the reference can be, quite simply, to separation in the form of abstinence (4.20), but it refers also to a degree of holiness, though its exact nature is not always clear (see, e.g., 2.22 (15) (two refs.); 2.27; 2.33; 4.31). Hence *perushim* can refer to those who are in a particular degree of holiness, as in 2.18, or in the singular 3.3, 4.3. In those passages there is no necessary suggestion that the *perushim* or the *parush* are members of a single, organised group. In other words, there is not necessarily any sectarian or partisan implication here at all, any more than there is in the Tannaitic passages referred to above. However, there are some collective uses of *perushim* which do seem to refer to an identifiable group or at least to people in an association with each other of sufficient coherence for their views or attitudes to be identifiable. It does *not*, however, follow that all such references are to the *same* group; in other words, even here it would be misleading to translate *perushim* as 'Pharisees'.

The clearest instances of a collective use of *perushim* (as referring to those who hold identifiable views) are those in which the *perushim* are involved in controversy, usually with the Boethusians or the Sadducees. Examples will be found in 2.38 and 3.19. Yet even here caution has to be exercised, because these references give virtually no details about the *perushim*, apart from the disputes in question; and in other passages, where the word *perushim* has a similar collective usage, the word appears to refer to extreme ascetics (3.11;

[1] It is possible that the same association of ideas underlies the command of God in 6.18.

4.26), without reference to any further organisation; indeed, if there are 'organisations' associated with the Ḥakamic/rabbinic tradition, they are the *ḥaburoth*, the formal groups with ranks or degrees of membership, which drew their members into increasingly careful observations of purity and holiness.[1] No comparable details for the organisation of the *perushim* can be found in rabbinic sources.

It follows from all this that there is no uniform use of *perushim* in the rabbinic sources, and that it cannot, therefore, be uniformly translated. More significantly, there is a certain conflict in the uses which occur: on the one side, it is clear that the term *perushim* was in fact used of the Ḥakamim, at least by their opponents, and that there are instances of the Ḥakamim and the *perushim* holding identical views over against the Sadducees; furthermore, it is perfectly possible for the term to have a good sense. Nevertheless, on the other side, the term is used more often to describe (sometimes to condemn) extreme separation, of one kind or another, and the *perushim* can be talked of in distinction from the Ḥakamim, as though a separate group. It becomes clear, therefore, that what has to be explained is a transition: a transition from an original situation, in which the name Pharisaioi/*perushim* was applied to an identifiable group (certainly by its opponents, but also by others on a sufficiently wide scale for it to appear as the unquestioned name of the group in Josephus), to a later situation in which the members of the group as it had vastly developed rejected the name and applied it to others in distinction from themselves. How did this come about?

The emergence and development of the Ḥakamic movement

In order to answer this question, it is necessary to trace – even though in briefest outline only – a possible interpretation of the emergence and development of the Ḥakamic movement. It is clear, both from Josephus and from the rabbinic sources, that fundamental in the Ḥakamic movement was a vision of holiness – a vision of implementing what God required of his people if they were to *be* his people. There is nothing surprising in the vision itself; it was shared by many other Jews. The real issue was how to achieve it: how is it possible for the command, Be holy as I am holy, to be implemented? Many of the divisions among Jews during the period of the second

[1] See further the discussion on pp. 35f.

commonwealth were in fact a consequence of different answers being given to that deeply basic question. On one point most would be agreed: that holiness requires separation from uncleanness and from anything which Torah defines as imparting impurity. But how is separation to be achieved? Does it require, for example, a literal geographical separation? The notion of a holy land might suggest it,[1] and some Jews took the suggestion even further, as in the withdrawal to the Dead Sea to create a particular 'holy community'. Concentration on a focus of holiness in the Temple was another form of geographical separation: even if contamination could not be avoided in the world at large, at least at one point, surrounding the Holy of Holies, sanctity could be preserved. A deeply important factor in bringing the Ḥakamim into being as a recognisable group appears to have been the belief that geographical separations of this kind could not lead *all* the people to fulfil the command of God. To put it the other way round, it is clear that the Ḥakamic movement believed that it should be possible for all the people to present themselves holy before God no matter where they lived: the proper enclave in which to live is within Torah itself, not in particular geographical isolations in which alone holiness might prove possible; hence, where others built walls on the shores of the Dead Sea, or within the Temple, they built a fence around Torah (2.26; 2.27).

This emphasis at once explains two fundamentally important characteristics of the Ḥakamic movement, their initial identification with, and influence over, the ordinary people, and their development of exegesis of Torah. The two in fact belong together. If all the people were to achieve holiness as Torah defines it, it was essential that the definitions of Torah should be both intelligible and applicable. That they should be intelligible led to the wide extension of education, and of the synagogue itself, in the Ḥakamic movement;[2] that they should be applicable meant a vigilant and ever-recurring attention to the ways in which the written and given text of Torah could be brought to bear on situations or circumstances which had not obtained at the time of Moses.[3] The circumstances were often

[1] Conversely, the uncleanness of the lands of other nations (formally enacted in the first century B.C.E.) would also suggest it: see 4.4, and cf. also 9.3.

[2] On the emergence of synagogues, see Bowker, *The Targums and Rabbinic Literature*, Cambridge, 1969, pp. 9ff.

[3] For an example, see 2.3. For a fuller discussion of the methods and consequences of rabbinic exegesis, see the Introduction to *The Targums and Rabbinic Literature*.

those which actually occurred, but equally, attention was given to circumstances which *might* occur – hence the juxtaposition of both actual and theoretical considerations in rabbinic works. Eventually, highly detailed methods of exegesis were developed, but these only gradually emerged.

It is thus fundamental for the rabbinic attitude, as Allon has observed, that all men should be in a state of ritual purity.[1] For the Ḥakamim, the issue was basically whether purity could be attained *in via*, in the world of ordinary commerce and existence. For this reason, Allon argued that there were two fundamental aims, or principles, governing the Ḥakamim:

'One was to make halakah accord with the needs of the living, and the other was to extend holiness (*qedushah*) to every man (not only to the priests), and to every place (not only to the Temple), and to every moment of time. The second principle made it necessary for the Ḥakamim to teach ritual purity to Israel and to demand complete separation.'[2]

What united the two principles was the belief that Torah, if given by God, must be able to be kept. If one knew what the Law *meant*, he would know how to keep it. Hence arose the extreme attention to exegesis – not simply to a proliferation of private interpretations, but to a controlled and well-ordered exegesis.

The basic obligation of searching out the meaning and application of Torah was no easy matter. It was assisted by the recognition that Torah had already been applied and 'lived out' by earlier figures from the time of the prophets, pre-eminently exemplified in the restoration of Torah under Ezra. Thus the notion of 'Scripture' was as important as the acceptance of Torah, since within the writings coming from the later period, the first interpretations of the meaning of Torah could be found. Yet of course there was no reason in principle to stop at Ezra. In practice it proved necessary, not least because of the proliferation of 'scriptures'; but in fact the important point was that the earlier writings recorded the first implementations of Torah, and tradition continued the record in the 'post-scriptural' period. From this point of view, the long tradition of what it has

[1] G. Allon, 'The Application of the Halakoth on Purity', in *Researches in the History of Israel*, Tel Aviv, 1957, I, 148–77 (Hebrew).
[2] *Op. cit.* p. 176.

meant in practice to obey Torah (and equally to disobey Torah) is in a sense as important as Torah itself. Torah and Scripture have a distinct status, but the tradition of what Torah means in practice continued to be an essential part of exegesis. Thus when the Sadducees denied the validity, both of the methods of Ḥakamic exegesis, and of the support which they gave to traditional ways of doing things, and when they insisted on the application of the literal text of Torah wherever possible, they were in fact creating another isolation – in addition to the geographical isolation of the Temple as an enclave of holiness, they were in effect isolating Torah from the lives of most people, since it was not in fact possible to apply the literal text of Torah without interpretation.

The fundamental vision of holiness, and of all the people implementing that most basic command of God, makes it entirely appropriate that the Tannaitic sources, as referred to on p. 14, should define *perushim* in terms of holiness. But how precisely the Pharisaioi/Ḥakamim emerged is uncertain – not enough evidence has survived. On one point, Josephus and the rabbinic sources are in agreement, though for different reasons, namely, that no precise date can be given for the emergence of a distinct 'party' or 'sect'. From the rabbinic point of view, this is simply because the Ḥakamim do not represent a sect: they represent a stage in the transmission of the intended interpretation and application of Torah, which goes back to Moses. For this reason, the chain of tradition is constantly referred to, and the methods of rabbinic training carefully perpetuated it (e.g., 2.26; 3.18; 4.22; 3.5 and 5.6); equally, it is for this reason that the rabbis themselves endeavoured to trace the point at which traditional interpretations of particular points in Torah first came into being (see, for example, 3.13, 5.9, 9.4 (Ezra); 4.24 (Haggai); 4.4 (Solomon)). If the Ḥakamim have the appearance of being a 'party among parties', it is primarily, from the rabbinic point of view, because aberrant or deficient interpretations of Torah were practised in the period before the fall of the second Temple, and the Ḥakamim were compelled to resist them.[1] Although this point of view is over-simplified, it at least serves as a reminder that

[1] The serious consequences of division are noted in 5.17. Many non-heretical 'groups' also existed: see, e.g., 2.13, 2.20, 2.22, 5.7, 6.8; and note also 'the sons of the synagogue'. It is precisely because the Ḥakamim identified their vision, or intention, with the whole people that Baeck could argue that the Pharisees 'were not a party . . . or yet a school or sect . . . but a movement within the Jewish people' (*The Pharisees*, New

the roots of the Ḥakamic vision go very far back, and that the Ḥakamim are, in their own circumstances, an application of principles implicit in Torah itself, and certainly exemplified in the prophets. Why, then, did they become identifiable as a separate group with their own procedures and principles of organisation?

The immediate answer is because they had to do so. To that extent, it is probably no coincidence that the first incident in which Josephus used the name Pharisaioi (though it is not the first mention of the name) is the incident which led Hyrcanus to expel the Pharisaioi from participation in the counsels of the state, despite the fact that previously he had implemented a number of their interpretations (1.2 (296); 1.4 (408); 2.4; 2.22 (10); 3.10; 4.23). Furthermore, it is the first incident, chronologically, in which Ḥakamim and *perushim* are associated in the rabbinic sources. It seems, therefore, likely that while the proto-Ḥakamic movement had been gathering momentum long before this time (and may, therefore, as has often been suggested, be connected with the Ḥasidim of the Maccabean revolt; on this, see the discussion in W. Beilner, 'Der Ursprung des Pharisäismus', *B.Z.* III, 1959, 235ff.), the necessity to become a distinct party originated in the time of John Hyrcanus, precisely because they were excluded from direct participation in government – and hence from the possibility of implementing their vision from the centre.

If this is so, it suggests that the emergence of the name Pharisaioi/*perushim* also dates from this period, and that it had, as has long been suggested, a good and a bad sense. Applied to the Ḥakamim as those who were separating themselves into a self-contained community – albeit, a community in the world – it meant 'separatist' in a derisive sense. But the title could be tolerated, perhaps even be gratefully accepted, since it also had two perfectly good senses: the first, as has already been examined, connects the name with holiness. The other connects the name with exegesis, since the root letters, *prsh*, can also bear the meaning 'interpret' or 'interpretation' (see, e.g., 8.1; 8.5; 8.7).[1] There are a few surviving hints that this meaning

York, 1947, pp. 11f.). There were organisations *within* the Ḥakamic movement, and there were extensive methods of control, but these did not amount to a sectarian organisation.

[1] The meaning 'interpret' has a Biblical foundation: see, e.g., Lev. xxiv.12, Neh. viii.8. Note also 'the Name to be interpreted' which may carry with it the sense, 'the Name to be utterly separated' (from uncleanness). See M. Reisel, *The Mysterious Name of Y.h.w.h.*, Assen, 1957, pp. 77ff.

was attached to the Pharisaioi. This is specifically the case in Yosippon, in the translation of the episode in which Hyrcanus expelled the Pharisaioi/*perushim*. In Yosippon, a clear connection is made between Ḥakamim and *perushim* (ed. Hominer, p. 111. ll. 9 and 10; p. 119, l. 26 (1.3)), and in the appended note (6.20) the name is associated with the meaning 'interpret'. But the problem of Yosippon is to know the value of its historical reference.

Similar problems complicate a comparable reference in ibn Shahin's *Book of Comfort* (ed. J. Obermann, N. Haven, 1933, pp. 107f., MS 93a/b), in which the name appears to be connected with interpretation. But quite apart from the problem of the provenance of the reference, there are equally great textual problems, which Obermann summarised as follows: 'Editing, critically, an Arabic text from a single manuscript written in Hebrew characters and removed from the authentic text-form of its author by a period of perhaps half a millennium and by the accumulated errors of who knows how many copyists is virtually an unending task' (p. xiv).

Despite the difficulties involved in these two passages, it is possible that they are not simply a later interpretation of the name, but that they preserve an authentic tradition which connected *prsh* with interpretation. There are also some surviving hints of a connection between *perushim* and interpretation in rabbinic sources, but they are by no means unequivocal. The clearest is perhaps 6.2, the account in the second version of A.R.N. of the origin of the Sadducees and the Boethusians. It is possible that the account intended a deliberate play on words, that while both Ḥakamim and Sadducees are *perushim*, the Ḥakamim are so because they accept interpretation of Scripture, the Sadducees are so because they do not. A similar connection between Ḥakamim and *prsh* 'interpretation' may also underlie Hillel's famous summary of obligation to the would-be convert, in 4.6.

It follows that even if the name *perushim* was intended derisively, it was nevertheless tolerable, since it could be converted to illustrate important truths.[1] Furthermore, it seems likely that it *had* to be tolerated, since the opponents of the Ḥakamim were in fact using it,

[1] It should also be borne in mind that the term 'separatist' with reference to holiness would not *in itself* be unacceptable. Note also the patristic tradition which accepted that √*prsh* conveyed a sense of separation, but referred it to schism among the Jews: references will be found in E. Schurer, *A History of the Jewish People*, Eng. tr., Edinburgh, 1898, II. 2, pp. 20f.; for an example, see 9.9.

and it did become of such universal usage that it was the obvious name for Josephus to adopt. It remains possible that the Ḥakamic movement did not refer to itself in general by any name at all, but that it reserved its names for particular functions within the implementation of its interpretation (and vision) of Torah. It has to be remembered that the *intention* of the Ḥakamic movement was to extend its interpretation of Torah (and hence the possibility of holiness) to all men. In *theory*, therefore, the extent of the Ḥakamic movement was coterminous with the Jewish people, and it must be remembered that many different people, in different occupations (including priests) belonged to the movement: to have given it a separate name would have been to suggest that the Jews could in fact be divided in their understanding of Torah. Even those who had particular functions within the movement, as, for example, those who were trained in the interpretation of Torah and in the transmission of those interpretations, pursued other occupations as well – as Paul carefully pointed out in his own case.[1] The movement was not intended to be a party within Israel. It was intended to be Israel itself.[2]

To a remarkable extent, that vision came true after the fall of Jerusalem, when the rabbinic continuation of the Ḥakamic achievement became by far the most dominant expression of Judaism. In the earlier days, it was not always so. After John Hyrcanus excluded the Ḥakamim/Pharisaioi, they were compelled into a degree of isolation. They could nevertheless continue to extend and implement their interpretations of Torah because of their direct contact with the people. It also seems likely that they became increasingly influential in courts of law, for a pragmatic reason. Here, the connection of Scribes (*sopherim*) and Ḥakamim is of great importance. The Scribes, in origin, were transmitters of Torah, not only in written form, but also in courts of law. The task of the Scribes in the latter respect was to produce those parts of Torah applicable to the case in hand. Obviously, Torah is not unambiguous, and to a limited extent the Scribes were compelled to interpret Torah – hence the

[1] Acts xviii.3, and cf. Acts xx.34, I Thess. ii.9, II Thess. iii.8; cf. 6.8.

[2] Hence Allon argued ('The Relation of the Perushim to the Authority of Rome and to the House of Herod', *Zion*, IV, 1938, 300–22; reprd. in *Researches in the History of Israel*, Tel Aviv, 1957, pp. 26–47; the article is in Hebrew) that the Pharisees were concerned, not only for specifically religious matters (so far as they can ever be detached), but for the proper ordering of the whole of society: see especially p. 303.

dibre sopherim, the words of the Scribes, which became as binding as Torah itself (see 2.24 and the further references). But it was a conservative approach to interpretation; furthermore, the scribal approach, by returning on each occasion to Torah, excluded the conveniences of case law – in a sense, each case had to be argued from first principles. The attractive merit of the approach of the Ḥakamim was that it accommodated case law within its understanding of the importance of tradition. The Ḥakamim insisted, as emphatically as the Scribes, that the application of casuistry must in principle be able to be taken back to Torah, but they were prepared to work from the endpoint of the development of case law within the living tradition, provided that the sub-structure could be guaranteed.[1] It is precisely because they had to be certain of the trustworthiness of the chain of tradition that the procedures of transmission within the Ḥakamic movement, in terms both of method and of training, came to be so elaborately and so rigorously developed.

The exact extent of the influence of the Ḥakamim in courts of law is impossible now to determine; but what is certain is that the Ḥakamim gradually displaced the Scribes in their role of interpreters of Torah.[2] This relation between the Scribes and the Ḥakamim explains why, in the rabbinic sources, the Scribes and the Ḥakamim are, in some places, separate groups, and yet the names are, in other places, used interchangeably, as though there is no distinction, so that the term *sopherim* does apply to the Ḥakamim. The situation is further complicated by the fact that while the Scribes retained their function as transmitters of the text of Torah and as writers in general, but were largely displaced by the Ḥakamim as interpreters, they could, like anyone else, join the Ḥakamic movement, and even become Ḥakamim.[3] Thus in some instances Ḥakamim and Scribes *are* as a matter of fact identical. The transition in the role of the

[1] The importance of *halakoth* being able, if necessary, to be taken back to Torah can be seen in 4.22, since it was a control on innovation. This was one of the issues between R. Aqiba and R. Ishmael, and their respective 'schools' of exegesis: see *Targums and Rabbinic Literature*, p. 54.

[2] The conservative and limited nature of scribal exegesis is recognised in 2.30; cf. 2.36, 4.21. But the *authority* of that exegesis was emphasised.

[3] Amongst many examples, see, e.g., the description of R. Meir in B.Gitt. 67a. It follows also that the *sopherim could* be *perushim*, and in places their views are identical: see especially E. Rivkin, 'Defining the Pharisees', p. 213. This is of great importance in considering the Scribes in Mark.

Scribes had begun before Jesus was born, and it is of interest that the references to Scribes in Mark, and some of the references in the other synoptic gospels, reflect the detail of this transition with great precision.[1]

We have seen, so far, that although the Pharisaioi/Ḥakamim were excluded by John Hyrcanus, they nevertheless continued to extend their influence. The very fact that they denied a geographical isolation, as indispensable for the attainment of holiness, meant that they could establish their principles and their interpretations far beyond the borders of Judaea – hence the very strong communities which grew up in Babylonia. The Ḥakamic movement had a life and continuity of its own, whether or not the over-riding authorities in power at any moment accepted or persecuted it. The actual moments of central power were few – and for that reason memorable; thus when Salome Alexandra reversed Jannaeus' persecution of the Pharisaioi and brought them into her counsels, the two great Pharisaic leaders of the time, Simeon b. Shetaḥ and Judah b. Tabbai, were able to implement important provisions (4.4 and the further references), and the reign of Salome Alexandra was remembered by the rabbis as a golden – almost a messianic – age (e.g., 6.5).

It follows that the Ḥakamic movement was able to exert a strong influence, even when excluded from actual or institutional power, because of the wide base of its popular support. We have already seen an example of this in the way in which the Ḥakamic interpretations of Torah were implemented in the Temple, even though probably the majority of the priests disagreed with them. Another, and more important, example of the way in which the Ḥakamic movement was both integrated into the constitutional life of the country, and yet was frequently in fact isolated from it, can be seen in its relation to the Great Sanhedrin. If, as seems likely, the Ḥakamic movement was able to extend its influence through its practical usefulness in courts of law, an even greater possibility of influence, at least in theory, was offered through the Great Sanhedrin.

Like much else in this period, the origins of the Great Sanhedrin are obscure. As in the case of Pharisaioi/*perushim*, there is a conflict between the Greek and the Semitic sources. In the Greek sources,

[1] See further *Targums and Rabbinic Literature*, pp. 54ff. I have also completed a study of the Scribes in the Gospels, which I hope it will prove possible to publish.

the Sanhedrin (not necessarily described as Great) appears predominantly as a judicial and also political body (it is, for example, before the Sanhedrin that Herod was summoned, according to Josephus (1.6, 1.15)), and these also appear to be its principal roles in the New Testament. But in the rabbinic sources, its functions are much more specifically religious: it is the final court of decision – and of appeal – in matters which are indispensable to the functioning of Israel as a people before God, as, for example, in accepting the witness of the new moon (on which the calendar and subsequent feasts depended), or in judging the rebellious elder (the trained and knowledgeable teacher who persisted in his own opinion even when the lower courts had ruled against him). According to the rabbinic sources, the Great Sanhedrin is the supreme court at the head of a number of approach courts, but, according to the Greek sources, there are a number of sanhedrins, which people such as Herod or Gabinius could call into being if they so desired (1.5).[1]

The solutions which have been proposed to the apparent conflict of evidence are almost innumerable, ranging from arguments that the rabbinic sources are totally hypothetical (giving a picture of what they believe ought to have been the case rather than what was actually the case) to arguments that the Greek sources were not interested in the religious role of the Great Sanhedrin and therefore distorted the picture; or again, it has been argued that there were two separate supreme sanhedrins, one in judicial, the other in religious, matters; or that the Great Sanhedrin was simply a religious 'committee' of the main Sanhedrin, the main Sanhedrin being actually more important in the administration of justice (hence the Greek sources), the religious Sanhedrin being theoretically more important (hence the rabbinic sources). What seems likely is that the Great Sanhedrin had an ambivalent role, partly because it is most likely to have become important as a part of the solution to the constitutional and religious crisis posed by the

[1] The clearest introduction to, and summary of, the rabbinic understanding of the Sanhedrin is that of Maimonides, as translated in the Yale Judaica Series (III, *The Book of Judges*, trs. A. M. Hershman, Yale, 1949) and read in conjunction with the notes which indicate the sources of Maimonides' information. The two main, and indispensable, studies of the Great Sanhedrin are those of S. B. Hoenig, *The Great Sanhedrin*, New York, 1953, and H. Mantel, *Studies in the History of the Sanhedrin*, *H.S.S.* XVIII, 1961. Note Urbach's criticism, 'Class-Status and Leadership', pp. 51f.

Hasmonaean determination to take over the high priesthood. Reference has already been made to the crisis and to the compromise solution which was reached in the case of Simon.[1] According to the decree in I Macc. xiv.28, the issue was so important that it required the calling of the supreme (and probably quite rare) assembly of the time, the Kenesset haGedolah of the rabbinic sources.

The calling of the Great Assembly to ratify the Hasmonaean settlement raises the question of the nature of the Great Assembly – and it is this which suggests a possible connection with the Great Sanhedrin. It has often been assumed that the Kenesset haGedolah was a national assembly, or perhaps a 'college' of experts founded by Ezra, which met irregularly on occasions of difficulty or of great crisis.[2] But in Aboth i.1 (2.26), the men of the Great Assembly (Synagogue) are part of the long chain of tradition from Moses to the present, standing between the prophets and the *zugoth* (the pairs of Ḥakamic leaders); and according to A.R.N. i, B.Ber. 33a, B.B.B. 15a, J.Sheq. v.1, the achievements of the men of the Great Synagogue had a closer relation to the regulation of community life than to actual political decisions: they canonised some of the later books; they classified *torah shebe 'al peh* (Torah transmitted by word of mouth) into *midrash*, *halakah*, and *haggadah*; and they instituted various prayers and benedictions. On these (and on other) grounds Finkelstein argued that the Great Synagogue was not an official, national assembly, convened in times of great crisis, but that it was a non-official grouping of those who were religiously concerned, from the time of Ezra onwards, to resist the extension of the high-priestly authority and decisions; the regular assembly in relation to the high priest would then be the *gerousia*, the council of elders.[3] But from either point of view the power and influence of the Great Assembly are obvious from its role in the Hasmonaean settlement. What is therefore significant is that both the Great Assembly and the *gerousia* from this point on, begin to disappear, and that the Sanhedrin begins to emerge for the first time (though not necessarily defined as 'great'). The general effect of the Bet Din or Sanhedrin was to limit the powers of the high priesthood in its new (and strictly

[1] See p. 9.

[2] On the 'Great Assembly', see particularly H. Mantel, 'The Nature of the Great Synagogue', *H.T.R.* LX, 1967, 69–91.

[3] L. Finkelstein, *HaPerushim weAnshe Keneset haGedolah*, New York, 1950, pp. 31ff.)

anomalous) form: the high priest's jurisdiction in the Temple was accepted and was combined with his political concerns, but matters indispensable to the life of the whole community became 'reserved business' – that is to say, they were taken away from the high priest and reserved for the new sanhedrins. The supreme of these sanhedrins was the Bet Din haGadol, but quite clearly not to the exclusion of lower courts, dealing with more local matters. At the same time, references are also made (e.g., M.Ket. i.5, T.San. iv.7, B.Pes. 90b) to the *Bet Din shel Kohanim*, the court of the priests. This court had jurisdiction in matters concerning the priests, as, for example, in examining the genealogy of claimants to the priesthood.[1]

A reasonably clear picture begins to emerge: the recognition of Simon as high priest was on any showing unacceptable to strict purists, who registered their dissent in various ways. But those who were prepared to adjust to the situation, as it had come to pass, produced a solution which allowed Simon (and his family) to act as high priests, but which reserved away from them matters of highest importance in the regulation of the community as the people of God. The fact that there was both a high priest and a priestly court meant that the Great Sanhedrin could be open to wider membership, and this undoubtedly gave to the Ḥakamim an opportunity of real influence and power.

The solution to the constitutional crisis of the Hasmonaean period worked well while the situation for which it was devised continued – while, that is, the Hasmonaean succession continued. But when it broke up in civil strife, and when Herod eventually succeeded, a totally different situation obtained. Quite apart from the new presence of Rome, the high priesthood reverted to appointment and to the possibility of subsequent family succession – hence the number of high priests and high-priestly families which emerged in the post-Herodian period. In the new situation, the Great Sanhedrin was theoretically anachronistic, since the anomalous situation for which it was intended no longer obtained. In fact, anomalies did not diminish in Herod's case, and the Great Sanhedrin continued; probably, in any case, it was too well established to be dissolved. It could, however, be *ignored* – or at least, attempts could be made to ignore it, by those who had no wish to submit to its judgements.

[1] Several other Courts are also mentioned in the pre-fall of Jerusalem period – including the Bet Din of the Hasmonaeans (B.San. 82a, B.A.Z. 36b). See, e.g., 2.20, 2.23.

In dramatic terms, this is obviously true of the sect of the Dead Sea Scrolls, since it did not accept the ordering of the calendar and feasts in Jerusalem, which was ultimately a matter under the jurisdiction of the Great Sanhedrin; but it is clear also that Herod paid as little attention to it as was possible in any matters which made any difference to his own plans; for this reason, it was more effective to summon a sanhedrin for himself than to try to work through, or with, an independent body which had had an existence prior to his own accession. The importance of the Great Sanhedrin thus undergoes a shift: it has a continuity of agreed function, at least in theory; but it becomes important primarily for those who *want* it to be important; it becomes effective for those who want it to be effective, so far as they can make it so – for those, in a sense, who want to give the skeleton, the basic structure, real flesh and blood. But those who wanted to give the Great Sanhedrin a more than theoretical importance are unlikely to be the same at every moment throughout the whole of the post-Herodian period. The shifts in political circumstances and alliances constantly altered the choices of action on the part of the various different groupings of Jews: the uses or otherwise of the Great Sanhedrin could thus be differently estimated at different times by different groups.

This at last begins to explain the apparent conflict between the Greek and rabbinic sources. The ambiguous status of the Great Sanhedrin (after the collapse of the situation for which it was devised) meant that it could be recognised as having authority in confined 'religious' matters, but that it could be circumvented or ignored when important matters of state were at issue; this, to a great extent, was the Herodian manoeuvre. On the other hand, the functions reserved to the Great Sanhedrin, which ensured its continuity in session, gave it a powerfully central position in relation to the community at large. It, therefore, contained within itself the potentiality of real importance in some circumstances, particularly in any circumstances in which a sufficient consensus *wanted* it to be important. Thus, it is not so much that the sources are in conflict, as that the conflict in the sources reflects a genuine conflict in attitudes.

This explains why the rabbinic estimate of the Great Sanhedrin combines both realistic and theoretical features. From the point of view of the Ḥakamim the Great Sanhedrin offered opportunities to put into effect their own position in several highly important areas of Jewish life. On the other hand, the effectiveness of the Great Sanhedrin was far from uniform; and even when it was in effective session, the Ḥakamim could certainly not guarantee being in a majority. Not surprisingly, they developed their own system of courts, scattered throughout important towns and centres, and leading up, at least in theory, to the Great Sanhedrin – the so-called 'approach courts'. These could implement the Ḥakamic position, even when the Great Sanhedrin was ineffective from their point of view. An equally important consequence of the ambivalent status of the Great Sanhedrin was the development among the Ḥakamim of a notional structure of authority within it, which persisted, even when the Ḥakamim were not actually in control of the Great Sanhedrin. This can be seen most clearly in the rabbinic records of the *zugoth*, the 'pairs' of ruler and vice-president (*nasi* and *ab bet din*) who presided over the Great Sanhedrin. In the unbroken chain of tradition, transmitting Torah from Moses down to the present, an important link is formed by the *zugoth*, Ḥakamic scholars, who, according to the rabbinic sources, held office continously from *c.* 160 B.C.E. (or perhaps later) to *c.* 10 B.C.E.[1]

There seems little doubt that, at least to some extent, the accounts of the *zugoth* are artificial, and that they had to be so. The five recorded *zugoth* cover a period of about 150 years, and (with the exception of the replacement of Menaḥem by Shammai (2.16)), they apparently held office coterminously – that is to say, they assumed and relinquished office at exactly the same time. When it is further realised that many of the *gezeroth*[2] or other decisions were transmitted on their own authority, without recorded reference to the Sanhedrin, it becomes clear that the theoretical and actual circumstances of authority did not always coincide – exactly the situation which Josephus in any case portrays. The obvious solution is that the emerging Ḥakamic movement saw in the Sanhedrin the opportunity for implementing their own interpretation of Jewish obligation and obedience to the commands of God. The Sanhedrin, however, was not always at their command. Nevertheless, the knowledge of what might be the case (particularly after the reign of

[1] For an introductory discussion and description of the *zugoth*, see A. Guttmann, *Rabbinic Judaism in the Making*, Detroit, 1970, pp. 33ff. For the terms *nasi* and *ab bet din*, see also *Targums and Rabbinic Literature*, p. 56.

[2] On this term see *Targums and Rabbinic Literature*, p. 41.

Salome Alexandra) made it necessary to keep alive a notion of continuous succession and leadership, even when these were not, as a matter of fact, being exercised by Ḥakamic leaders (except insofar as their authority extended over those who accepted the Ḥakamic point of view). Thus the assertion of Ḥakamic *zugoth* was never totally artificial, and on occasion the limited (partisan) authority of the *zugoth* was actually extended, when they were in fact presiding over the Sanhedrin, and when the Sanhedrin itself contained a Ḥakamic majority.

Divisions among the Ḥakamim

In the preceding section, it has been argued that the Ḥakamic movement consolidated round a fundamental and basic vision of extending holiness, and the real possibility of holiness, to all men.[1] In pursuit of this, they attended in great detail to the exegesis and interpretation of Torah, in order to establish its practicable meaning, and they took specific care to extend to the people (particularly through education and the synagogue) as much knowledge of Torah and of its interpretation as they could. Because of their close and (at least originally) sympathetic contact with the people, they gained extensive influence with them and received considerable support from them, though this was not necessarily signified by formal membership of such organisations as *ḥaburoth*. The Ḥakamim offered a serious possibility of 'holiness in the world', that is, of separation from uncleanness, as Torah requires it, even in the circumstances of ordinary life. In this sense, the Tannaitic sources, to which reference has already been made, were entirely justified in defining *perushim* in terms of holiness. But this simply re-poses the basic question: how then did it come about that a transition occurred from a possible good sense of *perushim* to the condemnatory sense of *perushim*, used to describe extreme separatists of one sort or another? An important part of the answer to this lies in the fact that even with the Ḥakamic methods of interpreting Torah, and

[1] The extreme stress on holiness is particularly clear in 6.21: the disciples of R. Neḥuniah wish to bring him back to earth from his trance and vision. Touching him with even the remotest degree of uncleanness is enough to break the connection between the holiness of God and the visionary.

of making its definitions of what holiness involves more possible for ordinary men and women, the actual achievement of a condition of holiness as defined in Torah was not easy. Thus it came about that although many ordinary people welcomed the support which the Ḥakamic movement gave to their customary and traditional ways (particularly in rituals which concerned them in the Temple), they by no means necessarily went further and accepted the whole detail of Ḥakamic interpretation in their own lives. This explains why, although it is abundantly clear (not least from Josephus) that the Pharisaioi/Ḥakamim took the side of the people in defending the validity of custom[1] and tradition as a legitimate means of understanding (and implementing) the intentions of Torah, the rabbinic sources contain violent attacks against the *ʿamme haAreẓ*, the 'people of the land' (4.22 and the further reference; see also the Index *ad loc.*); indeed, the term *ʿam haAreẓ* became virtually a way of referring to those who are careless about the obligations of Torah, particularly in matters of tithe (e.g., 4.23). This does not mean that the Ḥakamic vision of extending holiness to all men was diminished; on the contrary, it was, if anything, becoming stronger: for what in effect happened is that, whereas in the first place they were prepared to say, 'You shall be holy', they (or at least a part of them)[2] also went on to say, 'And indeed you *shall* be holy'; in other words, they insisted on the absolute necessity of holiness as indispensable for the people of God, particularly since the Ḥakamic principles and traditions of exegesis now made this unequivocally possible.

The reasons for the shift in emphasis from support among the people to attacks on the *ʿamme haAreẓ*, began to develop early on, and can be illustrated by two incidents concerning the ceremonies of Sukkot. Josephus frequently emphasised the support the Pharisaioi enjoyed among the people (e.g., 1.2 (298); 1.4 (401f., 406, 408); 1.12 (15, 17)), as also he frequently emphasised the importance to the Pharisaioi of tradition in the interpretation of Torah (e.g., 1.2 (296f.); 1.4 (408); 1.12 (12); 1.14 (110)). The two are combined in 1.3. Although the Pharisaioi are not mentioned by Josephus in his

[1] For the importance of custom, see, e.g., 2.7, 6.6, and see also *Targums and Rabbinic Literature*, pp. 43f.

[2] It is important to note Zeitlin's point, that the main antagonism was not between the *ʿamme haAreẓ* and the Ḥakamim/rabbis in general, but between the *ʿamme haAreẓ* and the *ḥaberim* (extremists in attention to purity and tithe, described on p. 35). See particularly 'The Pharisees, a Historical Study', *J.Q.R.* LII, 1961, 97–129.

account of the incident, 1.4 (401–2) suggests that Josephus believed the Pharisaioi were influential in it, as Yosippon states (see the reference in 1.3). In any case, the rabbinic sources make it clear that the Ḥakamim supported the customs in question (against the Sadducees), and they also preserve a memory of what is, almost certainly, this incident, even though it is, as so often, imprecise and Jannaeus is not named (2.12; 3.6; 4.15).[1] This is a good illustration of the Ḥakamic support of traditional and popular custom, which is not specifically named or ordained in Scripture. But on one occasion, when Sukkot fell on a Sabbath, the Boethusians forestalled the popular ritual of the willow-branches by putting heavy stones (on the eve of the Sabbath) on top of the branches collected for the ceremony: according to the prohibition on moving burdens on the Sabbath, the stones would not be able to be moved in time for the ceremony. The Ḥakamim supported the people in their assertion that the ceremony takes precedence over the Sabbath (which the Boethusians, of course, rejected, because they were doubtful about the custom anyway), but the people, the *ʿamme haAreẓ*, went even further and, disregarding the prohibition on moving burdens, moved the stones (3.5; 4.14; 5.6). This, in miniature, concentrates the essence of the alliance and yet of the tension which existed between the Ḥakamim and the ordinary people: the Ḥakamim went as far as possible to make Torah practicable for all the people, but they nevertheless insisted ultimately on the observance of Torah. The people welcomed the assistance of the Ḥakamim in alleviating the strictest interpretations of Torah and in defending their traditional ways, but many of them were by no means prepared to submit their lives to the whole detail of Torah – they had no real compunction about moving the stones.

This kind of tension, multiplied into other instances, helps to explain the development of conflict between at least the *ḥaberim* (and probably also some of the Ḥakamim/rabbis) and the *ʿamme haAreẓ*. It is equally important to realise that it produced conflict *among* the Ḥakamim, not so drastic, admittedly, nor of exactly the same kind, but serious, nevertheless. The issue among the Ḥakamim was created by the problem of knowing to what extent, or at what point, the ordinary people could be expected to understand and apply the detailed interpretations of Torah. Putting it in very general

[1] The later rabbis were aware of the problems of identification, as one can see from the discussion in 5.8.

terms, two different emphases were possible. On the one side, there were those who emphasised that the yoke of the law was easy and the burden light, since although the demands of God are sufficiently detailed to establish the distinction between obedience and rebellion, they are not impossible of fulfilment – since otherwise the terms of the covenant could never be met (e.g., 4.26); from this point of view, the first imperative was to encourage people to set themselves within the intention of keeping the covenant – after that, the details could be added as a constantly extending act of love towards God; and hence in this emphasis there was an interest in suggesting examples of the single imperative – the *kelal* which could be taken to summarise the whole of Torah.[1] On the other side, there were those, as mentioned earlier, who held that if the keeping of Torah was *not* an impossible imposition, then it clearly was meant to be kept; and in this emphasis the details were as important as the general spirit.[2]

This divided emphasis among the Ḥakamim did not drive them wholly apart from each other. Divisions and arguments among the Ḥakamim occurred on many issues, but more important than the divisions were the far greater unities of methods, beliefs and intentions which they held in common, and which differentiated them as a whole from, for example, the Sadducees or the communities on the shores of the Dead Sea. Thus, it was well-known that Hillel and Shammai were divided on several issues, as were their respective schools (Bet Hillel and Bet Shammai) after them. But they were divided within the same structure, not in isolation from each other.

Among the issues which divided Hillel and Shammai was the one under discussion, the priority of detail in the beginnings of the acceptance of Torah. This can be seen most clearly in the three stories of the would-be proselytes who came, on different occasions, to Hillel and Shammai (4.6). The stories indicate that in general Hillel adopted the former emphasis (the spirit of Torah embraced in a fundamental attitude, to which all else will naturally and as an act of love be added), whereas Shammai adopted the latter attitude (that the spirit of Torah is nebulous unless it is as a matter of fact

[1] On *kelal* see *Targums and Rabbinic Literature*, p. 51.

[2] So, e.g., in 6.11 each additional command is an additional opportunity for sanctification. The difference in emphasis is well illustrated in the contrasted understandings of the 'yoke of the kingdom' in 4.1 and 6.17.

expressed in its detailed provisions). The second story reveals the different emphases, since Shammai regarded the condition made by the proselyte as impossible, whereas Hillel summarised the basic stance of Torah, in his famous version of the 'golden rule', and then told the would-be proselyte that the rest of Torah is a way of coming to understand what it means 'not to do to your neighbour what is hateful to yourself'.

This anecdote is often quoted in isolation, but it is much illuminated by the two additional stories which form its context in the Talmud: the other two stories make it abundantly clear that although Hillel was anxious to encourage would-be proselytes to make a start in the faithful keeping of Torah (and to that extent held out more encouragement to them than did Shammai) it is to *Torah*, as interpreted by the Ḥakamim, that Hillel wishes to bring them – as indeed he must, since Torah is the God-given definition of what it actually means to love God and to love one's neighbour. Thus in the first of the three stories, Shammai's position is in effect that the written Torah is not self-explanatory, and that the tradition of its interpretation is *equally* Torah – and hence equally God-given, a position later to be stated in specific terms. Hillel's position is exactly the same – this is the unity in which the diversity between them was contained: his point is that the would-be proselyte cannot possibly understand or observe Torah on his own; just as he cannot know whether the alphabet goes, *a*, *b*, *c*, *d*, or *d*, *c*, *b*, *a*, without instruction, it follows that the would-be proselyte cannot rely on written Torah alone. The difference between Hillel and Shammai lies in the degree of their willingness to allow as proselytes those who will need to go through the long process of learning the alphabet of Torah, which in effect might mean large numbers, at any moment, of imperfect observers of Torah.

The third story illustrates a similar point, that Shammai, almost in principle, rejected the would-be proselyte's condition as absurd. Hillel, having made him a proselyte, then drew him further into the proper understanding of Torah, and at once the absurdity of his original condition becomes apparent to the proselyte himself. The proselyte's complaint against Shammai is that Shammai could have pointed this out without driving the would-be proselyte wholly away.

The three stories, taken together, illustrate very clearly the way in which there could be sharp distinctions among the Ḥakamim, but that they were distinctions within far more important agreements.[1] The divisions between Bet Hillel and Bet Shammai extended to many details of exegesis and interpretation. Bet Shammai usually adopted the more rigorous interpretation, where a matter was in dispute, and Bet Hillel the more possible of application – as one would expect from the three stories referred to above. Yet even here it is wrong to generalise, since there were instances of the reverse, of Bet Hillel being more stringent and Bet Shammai more lenient, as the rabbinic sources carefully note and record.[2] Eventually, the decisions of Bet Hillel prevailed;[3] in later theory, this was not because Bet Shammai had been wrong, but because the decisions of Bet Shammai were contained within those of Bet Hillel (4.8, 5.13). This is clearly an over-simplification, but it was an important point, theoretically, because it resisted the implication that *torah shebe'al peh* was simply a matter of opinion, not directed by God.

The tendency of Bet Shammai to be more rigorous in interpretation than Bet Hillel is of great importance in understanding the Ḥakamic movement and the forming of rabbinic Judaism. For one thing, it illustrates that the Ḥakamic movement was not an undifferentiated unity, but was much more like a stream in which conflicting currents flow along together.[4] Equally, it illustrates the

[1] It must nevertheless be emphasised that the arguments between the two schools caused divisions sufficiently serious for it to appear as though two Torahs (*toroth*) were emerging in Israel. In J.San. i.4(6) and T.San. vii.1 it is stated that the danger of schism was so great that local courts had to be established to deal with the proliferation of disputed matters; previously, 'law had gone forth to all Israel' from the Great Sanhedrin. For a collection of the original texts dealing with Bet Shammai and Bet Hillel, see I. Konovitz, *Bet Shammai–Bet Hillel . . .*, Jerusalem, 1965; and for texts, in translation, from the earlier period, see J. Neusner, *The Rabbinic Traditions about the Pharisees before 70*, Leiden, 1971, Vol. II.

[2] For references, see *Targums and Rabbinic Literature*, pp. 102f.

[3] Earlier, there had been occasions on which Bet Shammai had prevailed, as particularly over the implementing of the famous 'eighteen issues' (2.5). For references to Bet Hillel and Bet Shammai in the translated passages (where the points made here are illustrated) see the Index.

[4] It follows also that the Ḥakamic movement must be understood as a constantly developing growth, not as a static organisation. On this point, see particularly G. Allon, 'The Relation of the Perushim' (Hebrew), and A. Guttmann, 'Pharisaism in Transition', in *Essays in Honour of S. B. Freehof*, Pittsburgh, 1964. Note also J. Z. Lauterbach, 'The Sadducees and Pharisees', in *Studies in Jewish Literature: Issued in Honour of K. Kohler*, Berlin, 1913, where the connection with *Ḥakme Israel* is examined.

way in which a part of the Ḥakamic movement was pulled into increasingly elaborate detail in the observance of Torah and in the attempt to attain its definitions of holiness.[1] The same tendency can be seen in the development of the *ḥaburoth*. Exact details of the *ḥaburoth* and of the obligations imposed on the *ḥaberim* (members of a *ḥaburah*) are uncertain.[2] But in general it seems clear that these associations were developed to encourage individuals (and their families) to enter into increasingly scrupulous degrees of holiness.[3] There were ranks, or grades, within the *ḥaburoth*, and each of them represented a further advance in consciously accepted obligation.[4] Although all the details have not survived, it seems probable that the *ḥaburoth* were a movement within a movement, a kind of extreme deduction, drawn from the basic Ḥakamic vision (that holiness

[1] This is particularly clear in 2.15.

[2] See especially, as an introduction to the problems and discussion, J. Neusner, 'The Fellowship (*Ḥaburah*) in the Second Jewish Commonwealth', *H.T.R.* LIII, 1960, 125–42. Neusner concluded: 'J. Baumgarten, "Qumran Studies", *J.B.L.* LXXVII, 249–57, states: "All in all it seems quite difficult to make out of the *ḥaburah* anything more than a society for the strict observance of ritual cleanness." I have found no evidence to contradict Dr. Baumgarten's judgement. On the contrary, there is no indication that all Pharisees were members of a fellowship, although all members were Pharisees and accepted their views on Jewish law. There is, furthermore, no indication in the sources I have examined that the fellowship was an *organised* society at all, with officers or a formal governing body. A person became a member by stating his intention to keep the rules of the fellowship before three old members; he entered into the framework of obligations membership imposed. Membership thus entailed nothing more than a recognised status [i.e., 'nothing more' in addition to the obligations, about which there was a measure of agreement and progression, since otherwise membership of the *ḥaburah* would be virtually a private vow].' It should be noted that Zeitlin has argued that in origin the *ḥaberim* were citizens of autonomous cities, which would explain the Hasmonaean phrase *ḥeber haYehudim*, extending the status to the *whole* of Israel during the period of independence. Note also the connection of the *ḥaburah* with the provision of proper burial and mourning, in Semaḥot xii; it is of interest that Alexander Jannaeus connected the Pharisaioi with the provision of proper burial (1.4 (403f.)).

[3] See 2.2 and the further references.

[4] There are perhaps some indications of ranks, or grades, among the Pharisaioi in Josephus, in his use of the terms *demotikoi* (1.24 (197)) and *protoi* (1.23) in relation to the Pharisaioi. Cf. also 1.19 (411). It is possible that Justin's reference to Baptist Pharisaioi in the *Dialogue* (ed. Falls, p. 276) is a hint of divisions among the Ḥakamim, as argued in this Introduction, but the reference is too imprecise for any conclusions to be drawn.

should be possible for all men), which emphasised the progress possible in attaining the further degrees of holiness by its careful rules and ranks.

It is thus possible to discern, in several different ways, a basic tendency in a part of the Ḥakamic movement to emphasise, not simply that it is possible for all men to attain holiness, but that holiness, as Torah defines it in every detail, is what they *must* in fact attain, if they are to be parties to the covenant with God.

This suggests a very possible interpretation of the transition from an originally good (or at least tolerable) sense of *perushim*, to the condemnatory sense of extreme separatists. What appears to have happened is that a deduction, even more extreme than that of the *ḥaburoth*, was made from the Ḥakamic position – a deduction so extreme that it took those who adhered to it actually outside the limits of what the movement could contain. There are some indications that the Ḥakamic/rabbinic movement, or at least some members of it, began to characterise those who adhered to the extreme deduction from their own position as *perushim*. This does not mean that *all* instances of *perushim* have this reference, but that some may have it.

One of the clearest suggestions that this may have been the case occurs in the conflict between the description of the seven types of *perushim* in 4.22 and in 5.3 (the account in the Palestinian Talmud). It has already been pointed out that the account of the Babylonian Talmud describes the seven types in condemnatory terms (even though it is far from clear what all the descriptions originally meant). But the Palestinian account is *not* wholly condemnatory. At least the last two types are exemplified as good; and in the context of two unequivocally good types, it is arguable that the five previous types were intended originally to be understood as commendable. They can certainly be understood that way: at the worst, the descriptions are ambivalent, so that in an extreme form the behaviour described could be condemned, as in the Babylonian version.

In view of the contrast between the Palestinian and Babylonian versions, it is clear that the condemnatory use of *perushim* was not uniform, but that it gradually developed, at least in different areas, and perhaps at different times.[1] This is supported by the fact that even the condemnatory use in 4.22 is itself qualified by the addition

[1] Josephus was not himself uncritical of the Pharisaioi, despite his own allegiance to them and praise of them: see, e.g., 1.4 (409f.), 1.14 (111f.).

of a reminiscence of the advice which Jannaeus gave to Salome Alexandra (4.22 end). The danger envisaged in the passage is hypocrisy or pretence, but this is not yet attributed to the *perushim*: indeed, the *perushim* are *contrasted* with the hypocrites.

The passage is of importance, because it is a rabbinic memory (albeit abbreviated) of an incident in which Josephus used the term Pharisaioi and the rabbinic source used the term *perushim*, and the two are equivalent; furthermore the *perushim* are not condemned: it is the hypocrites, those who give the appearance of virtue while acting wickedly, who are condemned. Thus even the Babylonian version of the seven bad types of *perushim* has a qualification of the wholly condemnatory use. Furthermore, it suggests that the real danger of extreme observance was recognised by the Ḥakamim themselves as being hypocrisy, an attention to details of outward observance which concealed the realities of inward disposition.[1] This attitude is *not* attributed to the *perushim* in 4.22 (end) – exactly the reverse. But it *is* attributed to the *perushim* in 5.14: the two stories which illustrate the meaning of *makkot perushim* reveal a meticulous attention to the details of Torah which in fact defeat its real intention. This suggests the possibility that the later rabbis knew (as has been seen) that the term *perushim* had been applied to their predecessors, but they attributed the using of that term to their opponents (even the good use in 4.22 (end) is in the mouth of Jannaeus) – even though they knew that the term could bear a good sense. They themselves increasingly used the term to refer to those who were so extreme in their interpretations that they defeated the intention of Torah to help men to offer themselves and their world in holiness to God. This, in turn, suggests that the rabbis, and probably the Ḥakamim before them, recognised the dangers of extreme interpretations of their own positions and rejected them. Bet Hillel and Bet Shammai show that there could be distinction between rigorous and lenient interpretations; and the *ḥaburoth* are an indication that even more extreme deductions could be drawn in the endeavour to attain holiness, but the *ḥaburoth* were controlled and well-contained. The *perushim*, in at least some of the references, appear to refer to those who were so extreme that they took themselves out of the control of the rabbinic endeavour as a whole, and were attacked for doing so. This, of course, is not to deny that other

[1] As in 9.2. Note the attack on hypocrisy in the wearing of *tephillin* in Pes.R. xxii.5.

references, as has already been argued, may refer to 'separatists' who may not have had any particular connection with the Ḥakamim/rabbis in the first place; from this point of view, it is important to note Lieberman's argument that some references to *perushim* refer to those who desert the community in time of trouble (see 3.1).

Jesus and the Pharisaioi

The attack on *perushim* as extremists, and particularly on their attention to details of Torah to such an extent that the intention of Torah was defeated, and hence on their hypocrisy, is similar to some of the attacks on the Pharisaioi in the gospels. These are strongest (and very much more formalised) in Matthew and Luke, but they are present in Mark. In ii.16 the scribes of the Pharisees are criticised by Jesus when they express an attitude to the *'amme haAreẓ* (or perhaps to non-Jews) even more extreme than that of the Shammaites. In ii.18 extreme asceticism is condemned. In ii.24 an over-rigorous attitude to the Sabbath is rejected, as also, by implication, in iii.1ff. But by far the most specific reference is in vii.1ff., where an attack which is clearly related to the position held by the Ḥakamim in general (the emphasis on the importance of tradition) is made more specific by reference to the extremities to which it leads, and is in fact identified with hypocrisy.

The references to Pharisaioi in Mark are in fact extremely interesting, because they appear to reflect, with very great precision indeed, the transition from the Pharisaioi of Josephus to the *perushim*, attacked as extremists, of the rabbinic sources. Pharisaioi, as they appear in Mark, are certainly connected with the Ḥakamim (or with what is known of the Ḥakamim) as in the reference to tradition in vii.1ff., but they are more extreme than the Ḥakamim; in other words, they are already on the way to the positions condemned in the rabbinic sources. The connection with the Ḥakamim can also be seen in their concern with the same issues. For example, in some manuscripts (though not in all), the Pharisaioi raised the question about divorce (x.2): the argument expresses one of the viewpoints held by some of the Ḥakamim (the procedures and grounds of divorce being a well-known issue among the Ḥakamim themselves, and one of the debates between Hillel and Shammai). In this reference, the Pharisaioi are virtually indistinguishable from the

Ḥakamim. Similarly, in ii.24 there is no real distinction between Pharisaioi and Ḥakamim. The reference to the Pharisaioi being in the corn-fields reflects a deeply held principle which the Ḥakamim asserted against the Sadducees, that *limited* journeys on the Sabbath were permitted (the exact extent of the journey was a matter of dispute among the later rabbis, but not the principle itself, since otherwise country people or poor people would be less able to conduct their lives than the rich, because the houses of the rich would be much larger).[1] It is not in the least surprising – indeed, it is probably extremely accurate – to find Pharisaioi moving within the limit, since in many other controversies with the Sadducees the Ḥakamim went out of their way to assert their principles, particularly where these defended ordinary people against the prerogatives of the priests.[2] The offence, in this incident, lay in the nature of the work being done, not in the journey. It is possible that viii.11 is equally neutral in itself, but the reference is so integrated into the sign of the feeding that it cannot any longer be certain what the original meaning was, beyond a demand for credentials, comparable to the question about *exousia* (authority) at the beginning of the Gospel (i.21ff.). The associated reference in viii.15 is discussed below.

There are thus some passages in which the Pharisaioi are closely related to positions known to have been adopted by the Ḥakamim and subsequently by the rabbis. But there are also indications that they were more extreme than the Ḥakamim. A good example occurs in vii.3 and vii.5. The connection with the Ḥakamim (or more specifically with the Pharisaioi of Josephus) is clear from the references to the 'tradition of the elders' (vss. 3 and 5). But with regard to the washing of hands, the Pharisaioi here express a position more extreme than that of the Ḥakamim. Once again, the principle of hand-washing was important to the Ḥakamim, because it was a way of expressing an intention towards holiness comparable to the rituals of holiness in the Temple, but the exact extent (not the practice itself) of hand-washing was a matter of dispute among them.[3]

[1] For references to the Sabbath and to sabbath-journeys, see the Index.

[2] This is particularly clear in the deliberate insistence that the officiant in the ceremony of the Red Heifer must be in a state of *tebul yom*: see pp. 59–62.

[3] See 2.17 and the further references. Note that the very difficulty of *pugme* as a term may suggest the possibility that Mark was attempting to convey a technicality: for a summary of the many interpretations offered

The practices described by Mark are too extreme for at least the majority of Ḥakamim at this time, but they are by no means unlikely for Pharisaioi/*perushim*, in view of what is known of the extremist nature of *perushim* in the rabbinic sources. This is borne out by the reference in ii.18, which suggests that there was as close a connection between the Pharisaioi and the ascetic disciples of John the Baptist (at least in appearance and attitudes), as between the Pharisaioi and the Ḥakamim, despite the fact that the Markan Pharisaioi are undoubtedly related to the Ḥakamim. The asceticism suggested here is obviously comparable to the asceticism undertaken by some people in response to the fall of Jerusalem, whom the rabbinic sources call *perushim* (3.11, 4.26) emphasising an *increase* in numbers.

On this basis, it would be impossible (from the point of view of authentic historical reference) to find 'Scribes and Pharisees' associated together in an undifferentiated way. What one might find are Scribes as a term for Ḥakamim (i.e., as identical with the Ḥakamim), and yet also certain Scribes *associated* with the Pharisaioi, just as one finds in the rabbinic sources certain Scribes associated with the Ḥakamim, or with the courts, or even with the Samaritans, in addition to the use of *sopherim* as identical with the Ḥakamim. In other words, the Scribes were not themselves an undifferentiated movement, but were in the process of transition, in relation to the Ḥakamim, as has already been briefly described – and it is a point of interest that Mark's references to Scribes reflect that transition as accurately as his references to Pharisaioi reflect the transition to *perushim*.[1] Discrimination among the Scribes is exactly what one finds in Mark, as well as references to Scribes in general. In ii.16 the phrase 'the Scribes of the Pharisees' is precisely what one would expect (though not surprisingly attempts were made

(with his own suggestion based on a Latinism), see M. Hengel, 'Mk. vii.3, *pygme*: die Geschichte einer exegetischen Aporie und der Versuch ihrer Lösung', *Z.N.T.W.* LX, 1969, 182–98. On more general ritual cleansing as an issue between the Morning Bathers and the Perushim (3.19), particularly in relation to the status of *tebul yom*, see S. Zeitlin, 'The Origin of the Pharisees Reconsidered', *J.Q.R.* LIX, 1969, 255–67.

[1] See pp. 21ff. It is also important to note that many of the sayings of Jesus in controversy are equally accurate, in the context suggested here, often in a brilliant and subtle way. Even the supposedly mistaken reference to Abiathar (ii.26) can be seen as acute and highly penetrating polemic deliberately intended – but *only* while the Sadducaic/Zadokite claim was in being, and was being resisted; it would make little sense after the fall of Jerusalem.

textually to make the phrase less idiosyncratic, since the situation at the time of Jesus would not have been known at a later date). The phrase means, in effect, those Scribes who belong to (or support, or work for) the Pharisaic position or movement, as opposed to those who adhere to (or work for) other expressions of Judaism; and the incident reveals that they adopt an extreme Shammaite attitude to the non-Jew. Similarly, vii.1 makes a perfectly accurate distinction, not among the Pharisaioi, but among the Scribes.

It is thus not in the least surprising to find Pharisaioi in association with the Herodians, once they became certain of the need to oppose, and if possible put an end to, the teaching of Jesus. It would, perhaps, be odd to find the Ḥakamim in association with the Herodians, particularly in view of the earlier independence of (Josephus') Pharisaioi from Herod, and their refusal to take an oath of loyalty (1.9). But once the Pharisaioi became so extreme that they in effect removed themselves from the Ḥakamic movement (i.e., they became, or were on the way to becoming *perushim*), they no longer had the judicial or social means, so elaborately built up by the Ḥakamim, to enforce their position. Nor did they have access to the priestly courts, since their original connection with the Ḥakamim (and their continued adherence to Ḥakamic principles of exegesis and interpretation, extreme though they were in applying them) meant that they were necessarily separate from the priestly courts. The quite different system of authority established by Herod and by his successors offered an alternative way of opposing, and perhaps silencing, Jesus. The combination is first noted in iii.6, after an incident in which, typically, the Pharisaioi are much more extreme (but by no means improbably extreme) than the Ḥakamim in their attitude to the Sabbath; even Matthew seems to have been aware that the majority of Jews had a more generous attitude to the Sabbath, particularly in emergencies; but Matthew was not aware of the very subtle relation of the Pharisaioi to the Ḥakamim. 'Certain of the Pharisaioi and of the Herodians' are also associated in testing Jesus in Mk. xii.13. There is a hint in this passage of a recognised distinction between the Temple officials (xi.27) and the Pharisaioi, since although the assertion that the officials of xi.27 'sent the Pharisaioi' (xii.13) may be an editorial connection, it may also, possibly, reflect a situation in which the Temple authorities became concerned about Jesus (not simply because of the content of his teaching, but because of his insistence on teaching it in the Temple), but made use of a specific group (hence the force of *tinas* in this reference) to press Jesus further, because they were known (or even, though there is no evidence for this, because they had made themselves known) to be opposed to Jesus. In any case, it is not surprising to find Jesus warning against the secret and devious ways in which the Pharisees and Herodians work (viii.15); the reference has been integrated, together with viii.11f., into the account of the feeding of the multitude, but it is not difficult to discern and understand its underlying force: and viii.11 certainly underlines the way in which the Pharisaioi were concerned to identify the basis of his teaching and actions.

The offence and trial of Jesus

In view of the accuracy with which the transitional status of the Pharisaioi is reflected in Mark, it is wholly understandable that there is no reference to the Pharisaioi in the trial of Jesus. As has already been pointed out, their increasing dissociation from the Ḥakamim, and their existing dissociation (because of their *original* association with the Ḥakamim) from the priestly courts, meant that they were too small a minority to have an effective role in the courts, least of all in the Great Sanhedrin. What certainly *may* have happened is that they alerted others in authority to the dangers implicit in Jesus' position, without themselves being able to do much about it.

What, then, *was* the offence of Jesus, and why did anybody wish to take action against him?[1] Fundamentally, the offence of Jesus, so far as *jurisdiction* was concerned, lay in his attitude to the various sources of authority, since in many different ways he claimed and exemplified direct authority, and power, from God. Obviously, there were many 'false teachers' who were at most driven into exile, but they were not crucified: Judah b. Durtai might have to take himself away to the south, but precisely for that reason he was not crucified,

[1] Note that rabbinic Judaism came to form its own estimate of Jesus, in the light of subsequent history. The main (uncensored) texts are assembled, with comments, in H. L. Strack, *Jesus, die Häretiker und die Christen nach den ältesten jüdischen Angaben*, Leipzig, 1910; the longest connected Jewish accounts of Jesus occur in the Toledoth Jeshu tradition; for this, see particularly S. L. Krauss, *Das Leben Jesu nach jüdischen Quellen*, Berlin, 1902, and W. Horbury, 'A Critical Examination of Toledoth Jeshu', unpub. diss. Camb.

or executed (4.10). The greater problem of Jesus was that he insisted on the issue of the importance of what he was saying (and doing) by coming to Jerusalem and teaching repeatedly in the Temple.

But even then, what was problematic about the *content* of the teaching of Jesus? Not necessarily the same things for all Jews: for example, Jesus' acceptance of belief in resurrection would be welcome to the Ḥakamim, but not to the Sadducees (Mk. xii.18). What was particularly unwelcome to the Pharisaioi was his claim (as much in action as in word) that the action of God in the world of his creation can be made possible simply by the expectation, or faith, that it will be so, not necessarily by making that faith visible through the acceptance and observance of Torah, both written and interpreted. The contrast must not be made too extreme, since few, if any, even of the most extreme of those who insisted on the detailed observance of Torah believed that the relation of God to the world would be wholly broken until Torah was completely implemented: if that were so, repentance and the sacrificial system (to give but two examples) would make no sense. On the contrary, much thought was given to the ways in which God continued to relate himself to his people even though they were not wholly and completely expressing Torah in their lives. Yet the contrast, in the case of Jesus, was that he appeared to be claiming that the effect of God, the relation of God to a human situation, is possible even where no attempt at all is being made to accept and implement what God has commanded in Torah: sin can apparently be forgiven by a word (Mk. ii.1–12). Jesus did not necessarily deny the observance of Torah (note the preceding incident, Mk. i.40–4), but he certainly resisted the view that its observance is an indispensable and prior condition of the action of God; faith is, if anything, the prior condition.

The insistence on every detail of Torah as a prior condition is, as has been seen, an extreme deduction from the Shammaite tendency, which eventually took the *perushim* out of the Ḥakamic/rabbinic tradition; it must not, therefore, be identified with 'Judaism at the time of Jesus'. But equally the attitude of Jesus is, in a sense, an extreme deduction from the Hillelite tendency – so extreme that it eventually (or in fact quite rapidly) took Jesus and subsequently the Christians out of the Ḥakamic/rabbinic tradition as well; to become, in other words, a separate movement. Hillel had stressed, against Shammai, the importance of helping the would-be proselyte to take the first step.[1] But it was the first step in the same general direction as that of Shammai, towards the keeping of Torah as interpreted in the Ḥakamic tradition (though no doubt, more particularly, according to the interpretations of Hillel). Shammai perhaps wanted the proselyte to arrive there in one mighty leap, but the general objective, the keeping of Torah and of its traditional interpretations, was the same – this is the greater unity which contained their diversity. The extreme deduction of Jesus lay in his view that the first and only important step to be taken is in the direction of God. Thus his *kelal*, or summary, of Torah is the love of God and the love of one's neighbour as oneself: there is no greater commandment than these.

It is probable that originally Jesus was sufficiently close to the Hillelite tendency to believe that the expectation of God must first be established among the people whom God had chosen, before it could be extended to others; but his discovery that faith could be as real and as consequential among non-Jews as among Jews led to the obvious conclusion that the unity of effect between God and men is possible anywhere – indeed, greater faith can sometimes be seen among non-Jews than, ironically, among Jews who ought (in view of their history) to have been vastly more expectant of the action and effect of God.[2]

The basic issue was thus concentrated on what was necessary before the ancient and biblical (since both Jesus and his opponents appear to have accepted at least Torah in common as authoritative) covenant promises could come into effect. The Ḥakamim obviously held that the conditions as elaborated in Torah must be observed, although they were emphatic that every help must be given to men to keep those conditions. The (Markan) Pharisaioi/*perushim* insisted more extremely on every detail being kept, particularly since oral Torah made the details intelligible and possible. But Jesus was extreme in the opposite direction, and insisted that God was immediately possible, even when the detailed conditions of the covenant promises had not been kept. It is not the actions of men which create the actions of God, but the actions of God which create and transform the actions of men – or at least of those men who look to the actions of God with whole-hearted expectancy. In

[1] See p. 33.

[2] For a summary of the apparent conflict or shift in attitudes, see J. Jeremias, *Jesus' Promise to the Nations*, London, 1958.

this, as in almost all else, Paul, far from distorting the teaching of Jesus, expressed and continued it with great accuracy. Furthermore, since the verification of Jesus' assertions about the nature of God in relation to men could only ultimately lie in the relation of God to Jesus himself, and in the effect of God in his own case, it is not surprising that later reflection came to understand Jesus as a wholly real enacting and embodiment of the effect of God, and so, ultimately, as the incarnation of God.

The fact remains that although these claims would appear to be a betrayal of Torah, they were not necessarily a matter for crucifixion, particularly if Jesus had kept them to himself. There were many unorthodox teachers and sects around at the time, but scarcely any record survives of their having been crucified, and even then it may not have been for their teaching, or sectarian beliefs, alone.[1] The difference, in Jesus' case, lies in the fact that he did *not* keep his claims or teachings to himself, and that they were, in fact, deeply threatening, not simply to the principles of the Ḥakamim, or to the authority of the Temple, but to the basic structure of Jewish life as a response to God's gift of Torah to his people. So far as Jesus was concerned, Torah and the covenant may well have summarised the intention and the ability of God to be in precisely that kind of close relation, of promise and effect, with men (and conversely of men with God), but he clearly believed that the relationship could obtain, even when the details of the covenant, as specified in Torah, were not being kept; and this explains the radically disjunctive nature of a remark such as that recorded in Mk. vii.14f. But this threatened the very *raison d'être* of the Jewish people – *raison d'être*, in the sense that by accepting Torah, they could establish the conditions of holiness, by no means necessarily with a selfish intention for their own benefit alone, but on behalf of the whole world. Yet even so, granted that Jesus threatened this *raison d'être* and made it perhaps seem unnecessary, and granted also that he refused to be silent about it but asserted it in Jerusalem and even in the Temple precincts,

[1] E.g., Josephus *Ant.* xiii.380, *War* i.97; 4QpNah. 8. M.Eduy. v.6 (for the latter half see p. 70) records expulsion as the penalty for the 'rebel', but it also makes it clear that the death penalty (in these cases by stoning) was technically correct, even when it could not be implemented. For modes of execution in the N.T. period, see J. Blinzler, 'The Jewish Punishment of Stoning in the New Testament Period' in ed. E. Bammel, *The Trial of Jesus*, London, 1970, pp. 147–61, and E. Bammel, 'Crucifixion as a Punishment in Palestine', *ibid.*, pp. 162–5.

what could be done about it? In what way did the offence of Jesus make it possible to deal with him?

For those not themselves bound by Torah, some kind of direct action might have been possible. This might have evoked an angry response from those who had accepted as true what Jesus claimed about the possibility of God (and it must be remembered that if ordinary people welcomed, at least originally, the Ḥakamim, they might certainly, at least initially, welcome Jesus, though often, as Jesus observed, from dubious motives, and without serious intention to 'stay the course'; for this reason 'faith', as defined by Jesus, is a searching demand). But for those bound by Torah, that possibility was irrelevant (cf. 1.6 (167)). What had to be known, if Jesus was believed to be destructive of Torah, was in what particulars of Torah he offended. From this point of view, there is no need to doubt the urgency of the several different enquiries which Mark records. But the major category of offence into which Jesus appeared to fall was that of the so-called 'rebellious elder'.

The 'rebellious elder' is an ancient category, going back to Dt. xvii.12: it refers to the sane and competent person who refuses to accept the judgement of the highest court of the time in a matter which is admittedly difficult of interpretation. The procedure is so important for the preservation of Israel (because it ensures that ultimately, even in controversial matters, the opinion of the majority will prevail, and thus that there will not be private opinions in matters of Torah) that the man who refuses to accept the decision of the authorities of the time ('the judge who shall be in those days') must be executed; indeed, some of the later rabbis went further, and said that even if the condemned man retracted his opinion on the way to execution, he must still be executed, though other rabbis believed this to be too extreme.

But could Jesus be regarded as a 'rebellious elder'? As later defined, in clear and quite elaborate terms, by the rabbis, certainly not. The most convenient summary of the eventual rabbinic definitions of the rebellious elder is that of Maimonides, in the Treatise on Rebels in Book Fourteen of the Code (The Book of Judges). Ch.iii makes it emphatically clear that no one can count as a rebellious elder unless he

> 'repudiates the Oral Law as a result of his reasoned opinion and conclusion ... The rebellious elder of whom the Bible speaks is one

of the wise men of Israel who is at home in traditional lore, functions as judge, imparts instruction in the Torah as do all the wise men of Israel, but is in disagreement with the Supreme Court with regard to a question of law, refuses to change his view, persists in differing with them, gives a practical ruling which runs counter to that given by them.'

In terms of this definition, Jesus could not possibly count as a rebellious elder. But it is by no means certain that this definition was already established in full by the time of Jesus, and even though it was in the process of formation among the Ḥakamim, it certainly did not automatically obtain as a definition for those who were not a part of the Ḥakamic movement. This means that our uncertainty about whether Jesus might have been treated as a rebellious elder may be an exact reflection of the uncertainties of his contemporaries about who in fact counted as a rebellious elder. In a deeply divided situation, it might well appear to the Ḥakamim that various Sadducees were behaving like rebellious elders, by insisting on their erroneous interpretations; and no doubt the reverse was equally true. But the Ḥakamim and the Sadducees could scarcely proceed against each other on the basis of Dt. xvii.12, since in a situation of counter-balanced power there were no means of establishing one's own position as 'the judge in those days' over against the other. Eventually the rabbis *were* able to exclude the views they attributed to the Sadducees, and they did so in no uncertain manner, but that was long after the Sadducees had effectively disappeared. It may also be the case that the stories which record how certain Sadducees put their erroneous views into practice and were shortly afterwards struck dead may be more than moral and cautionary stories; they may also include an element that death was actually the appropriate punishment.[1]

It is thus obvious that in the divided situation which obtained before the fall of Jerusalem, it would be impossible to find an agreed definition of who counted as a rebellious elder, except insofar as a definition occurs in Deuteronomy, in which the culpable offence is a refusal to yield to the highest authority of the day. Apart from that, each reasonably coherent group, from the Sadducees to the sects of the Dead Sea, would define the phrase, and the authority of which he was in contempt, differently. Even for those who shared

[1] E.g., 3.4, 4.12, 5.8.

a general acceptance of central institutions (in this case, of the Great Sanhedrin), the divisions which obtained in the Great Sanhedrin, and which reflected the divisions of those who made up its membership, made it virtually impossible to act in a unified way against a nominal 'rebellious elder' – unless, of course, the Great Sanhedrin was dominated by one particular party; or unless a sufficient *consensus* of use could be obtained.

It is just possible that Jesus provoked the exploration of whether such a consensus of use in fact obtained. It is possible to interpret Mark's account of the final investigations into Jesus, which became in effect a trial, as an attempt to determine whether he might in fact count as a rebellious elder – with the clear expectation that if he *did* so count, the penalty, at least in scriptural terms, must be death. That there are confusions and apparent anomalies in the accounts is not surprising, since the procedures of the courts were in any case a matter of dispute in this period, and the later rabbis certainly knew of one capital case in which they believed an earlier court (which they explained as a priestly court) had acted anomalously at least in its method of execution (2.23 and the further references). But that this was not even intended to be a procedurally 'correct' trial (at least initially) is perhaps hinted in the phrase *en dolō*, in Mk. xiv.1; if the *killing* were not to be by stealth, then some basis for proceeding legally had to be established: could Jesus count as a (Deuteronomic) rebellious elder? From this point of view, the betrayal by Judas consists, not in the kiss, but in the word, Rabbi.

According to Mark the initiative in the investigation came from 'the chief priests and the scribes' (xiv.1; note also viii.31 (which adds 'the elders'), and x.32–4). It is uncertain whether the Scribes are those in association with the priests, or whether they are those who assist in a legal process, or whether the term is a way of referring to the Ḥakamim. The earlier distinctions among the Scribes in Mark make it likely that the phrase originally referred to those Scribes who worked with and for the chief priests, just as one finds, in rabbinic descriptions of the Great Sanhedrin, 'scribes of the court'. It is entirely possible, therefore, that the Ḥakamim had very little to do with the investigation of Jesus, and still less to do with setting it in motion. The real initiatives seem to have come from those in extreme positions, the *perushim* (in the sense that they alerted others to the possible dangers, as suggested on p. 41) and the Temple priests (to whom, in xiv.10, Judas went; note also xv.11), the former because they strongly rejected the destructive implications of Jesus' apparent way of by-passing Torah in arriving at God, the latter because of his insistence on asserting this understanding of God in the Temple. But in any case, it is only later (xiv.53 and 55), that reference is made to a larger group (using the term 'all', and including 'the elders'), though xiv.43 anticipates this, and suggests what may have been in mind.[1] In xiv.10 the initiative is still with the chief priests. So far as the session of the larger group, now referred to as 'the whole *synhedrion*', is concerned, it makes considerable sense to interpret this as an extension of the investigation (Mk. xiv.55b) to determine whether Jesus might count as a rebellious elder, with the priests taking the initiative. It is important to note that Mk. xiv.55 does not specify that they sought evidence of blasphemy on which to condemn him, but simply that they sought evidence (*marturia*) as a basis on which to proceed to execution. It is not surprising, therefore, that the *immediate* issue was concentrated on the extent to which Jesus had repudiated the Temple and, by implication, its authority. The precise form of the issue is no longer clear, perhaps, in part, because the tradition about the destruction and rebuilding of the Temple has been fused, in the Christian process of transmission, with predictions of the resurrection.[2] But that some issue involving the Temple was made fundamental undoubtedly makes sense, if Jesus was being investigated as a potential rebel (in the technical sense), since even the Ḥakamim strongly asserted the centrality of the Temple, even though they disagreed with much that went on there. It was thus a good test issue of allegiance and obedience. Equally, the stress on the conflict of witnesses[3] may well reflect an *original* uncertainty about whether he was to be counted as a rebellious elder, even though the conflict and the falsity of witness has come to have a quite different significance.

In the event, the uncertainty was resolved, not by a decision about his words (i.e., the content of his teaching) but by the confrontation between the high priest and Jesus. When the high priest challenged Jesus to respond to the evidence about his teaching and to clarify it himself, he still 'answered nothing'. This finally resolved the doubt, because the refusal of Jesus to participate in the proceedings of the

[1] On the 'elders of the court' cf., e.g., 2.11.

[2] For other examples of threats to the Temple, see E. Bammel in *The Trial of Jesus*, pp. 21ff.; and note the quite different personal involvement of Jesus.

[3] Mk. xiv.56ff.

investigation and to accept the decision of the majority on his teaching would constitute precisely that defiance which would define him, at least in a general way, as a rebel. The additional question of the high priest no doubt confirmed the correctness of this, by suggesting the additional offence of blasphemy, and certainly nothing further was needed from witnesses;[1] but the real offence of Jesus lay, not in the fact that he said 'I am', but in the fact that he said nothing. Silence was the offence, because it was a contempt of court which made him, in effect, a rebel against it.[2]

It seems likely that, in the conflicts and confusions, which the divisions among the Jewish parties made inevitable in the situation before the fall of Jerusalem, some doubts still in fact remained. Certainly, insofar as the Ḥakamic definition of the rebellious elder was in the process of formation, and insofar as any members of the Ḥakamim were included in this particular Sanhedrin, they would be unlikely to be wholly certain that Jesus did in fact 'qualify' as a rebellious elder. It is even possible to imagine Ḥakamim speaking, on technical grounds, in *defence* of Jesus, and resisting the consensus which the priests and those representing the *perushim* position were attempting to establish. The continuation of doubt would certainly explain the 'further consultation' of xv.1, and it may also help to explain why Jesus was taken before the Roman authorities. It is obviously possible to argue that this would have been necessary if the Jews, under the Romans, lacked the power to execute, though this is notoriously a disputed matter.[3] But (whether in addition to this or apart from this) the continuation of real doubt about the status of Jesus, as also about the anomalies of proceeding to a formal trial at this time, would make sense of the decision to take Jesus before the Romans, since in the circumstances then obtaining, it would suggest a quite different way of resolving doubts, by adding (or perhaps substituting) a political offence, just as the earlier session had in itself added the offence of blasphemy as confirmatory; and

[1] Mk. xiv.63.

[2] This interpretation would also make sense of the challenge to 'prophesy' in Mk. xiv.65: the only justification for a claim to be receiving direct authority from God would have been a manifest return of the spirit which inspired the prophets. See especially *Targums and Rabbinic Literature*, pp. 44f., and cf. I Macc. xiv.41, together with the discussion on p. 9.

[3] For a summary of this, and other points, see D. R. Catchpole, 'The Problem of the Historicity of the Sanhedrin Trial', in ed. E. Bammel, *The Trial of Jesus*, pp. 47–65.

for those who did *not* have any doubts, it would keep alive the possibility of dealing effectively with Jesus – and in this respect the attitude would be somewhat similar to that of the *perushim*, earlier, in attempting to proceed with the Herodians.

The main point of this argument is not to suggest that Jesus was arraigned as a rebellious elder according to the definitions and procedures which the rabbis later elaborated. This is certainly and unequivocally not the case. But the category of 'rebellious elder' long pre-exists the eventual definitions of the rabbis, since it originates in Deuteronomy; and in the process of moving towards the eventual definitions, there was much room for argument and uncertainty, particularly in a situation, like that preceding the fall of Jerusalem, in which conflicts of interpretation were in any case seriously divisive. If Jesus was approached as conceivably the kind of person envisaged in Deuteronomy, it could only be in this exploratory context of genuine conflict and uncertainty, in which consensus of action was not easy to obtain. It is at least a curiosity that this possibility enables Mark's account to be read in an entirely straightforward manner, since it makes sense of the confusions and apparent anomalies, which are necessarily a primary fact in the situation of the pre-fall-of-Jerusalem period. But even if this particular suggestion seems improbable (and it must inevitably be hypothetical, because of the paucity of direct evidence), the fact remains that in Mark the transitional nature of the Pharisaioi/*perushim* is very accurately portrayed. In Matthew and Luke this is occasionally the case, but both those gospels tend to generalise or 'explain' the references to Jewish parties; exactly the same is true of their references to Scribes, in which the accuracy of the portrayal in Mark is blurred. In John, the process towards artificial treatment is carried even further, and the term Pharisaioi virtually becomes a short-hand way of referring to 'those Jews who invariably opposed Jesus'.[1] It is by no means necessarily the case that the author of Mark was consciously deliberate in the accuracy of his portrayal. On the contrary, in view of the subtlety of many of the points, it is much more likely that he simply reproduced an accuracy which originated in the actual circumstances and which had not yet become disturbed in the transmission of individual traditions.

What this study suggests is that Jesus shared with the Ḥakamim

[1] See Bowker, 'The Origin and Purpose of St John's Gospel', *N.T.S.* XI, 398–408.

a mistrust of extremist tendencies in the Ḥakamic tradition, and that both attacked those tendencies with equal vehemence. Yet ultimately Jesus' insistence on the immediate reality of God to faith (linked though this is to the Hillelite tendency among the Ḥakamim) was too extreme for the Ḥakamim in the opposite direction, since eventually it led Jesus to the obvious conclusion that even Torah was less important than faith and the realisation of God to which faith can lead. There is thus a kind of interior logic which compelled Jesus to insist on the issue of what he believed to be the case about God, since if God is to be God as he claimed, the claim could only be asserted and verified in action and in life. It was thus an extreme part of the agony in the garden that the claim to the immediate reality of the effect of God was being brought to a real crisis; and if the effect of God was not to be manifested (as the later tradition elaborated) by angels or by the sword, then how *could* God be of effect, particularly if Jesus were to be, as he himself appears to have anticipated, killed? It is arguable that Jesus, in the limitations of his situation, was as anxious to know this as anyone else, and that this was a real part of the agony; for at the final moment of the crucifixion, it seemed that the effect of God *was* absent and that the claims of Jesus, about the nature of God and about the immediacy of the relation between God and man, were empty. Yet those who became the first Christians found that the effect of God was *not* absent, despite the extremity of dereliction, but that its nature, in the resurrection of Jesus, was startlingly unexpected. It was the resurrection which confirmed for them the validity of the way which Jesus had opened up to the reality of God, and which ultimately made it inevitable that Judaism and Christianity would become separated ways. Yet in terms of understanding how this came about, it is important to bear in mind how much Jesus owed to the Ḥakamic vision, even though he proceeded to its attainment by a radically different way: where Jesus evidently saw in Torah an exemplification of God's intention to be in a real and covenanted relationship with men, the Ḥakamim saw in the exemplification of Torah in the details of men's lives the only possible way to the reality of that relationship. But both at least believed that the relationship is possible and is intended by God, and that the final and ultimate danger lies in its frustration.

ADDITIONAL NOTE

Controversies against Sadducees and/or Boethusians

In the Introduction, reference was made (p. 10) to the importance of various controversies in understanding the attitudes of Jewish groups or parties in the period before the fall of Jerusalem. In some of the controversies against the Sadducees, the *perushim* are reported to have been the other party to the controversy. The controversies must necessarily be approached with caution, for two main reasons: firstly, there is sometimes an instability of names, so that in different accounts of the same controversy, the controversialists are, on occasion, differently named. But secondly, some of the controversies are extremely difficult to understand, particularly those which have been briefly recorded, or those to which only undetailed reference is made. For this reason, a brief description of the main controversies is given here. In no sense should these notes be regarded as a serious or adequate discussion; they are intended simply to clarify the main points of each controversy, so far as they can be discerned.

The controversies form an important part of Finkelstein's discussion of the Pharisees. The notes follow the order of his list of the controversies, though other classifications are equally possible and legitimate. Some of them are differently listed and discussed in Guttmann, *Rabbinic Judaism*, pp. 136–60. Finkelstein recognised that in some instances the Sadducees were not named, and that they can be regarded as the controversialists only by attribution. His list is as follows:

A. Ritual and juristic issues, in which a word or text of Scripture is disputed.

1. *'Omer* and the date of Shabuot.
2. The lighting of incense on the Day of Atonement.
3. The kindling of sabbath lights.
4. The Red Heifer and *tebul yom*.
5. Meal offerings and libations accompanying animal sacrifices.
6. Impurity of metals and glass.
7. The right of the daughter of a deceased son to inherit.
8. The treatment of false witnesses.

9. The responsibility of the master for damage done by his slave.
10. Ransom in place of execution.

B. Controversies involving the interpretation of the intention or spirit of Scripture.

11. Water libations and the beating with the willows at Sukkot.
12. Leniency in punishment.

C. Issues where Scripture is inexplicit.

13. The equal participation of all Jews in sacrifice: *tamid* and *sheqalim*.
14. The stream of *niẓẓoq*.

D. Customs admitted by the Ḥakamim to be post-Biblical.

15. Washing of hands.
16. *ʿErub*.

E. Priestly traditions opposed and condemned as Sadducean.

17. *Lex talionis*.
18. Manner of execution.
19. Impurity of a mother after child-birth.
20. Proof of virginity.
21. *Ḥaliẓah*.

F. Theological issues (notes have not been provided on these, since they are familiar and frequently discussed: see, e.g., S. W. Baron, *A Social and Religious History of the Jews*, Columbia, 1952, II, 35–46, for a brief introductory discussion. See also p. 12, n.1.

22. Resurrection and immortality.
23. Angels.

The following should also be noted:

24. The immersing of the *menorah*.
25. The writing of *tephillin* in B.Shab. 108a (4.7).
26. The witness of the New Moon (2.14 and the further references).

1 *'Omer* and the date of Shabuot (2.29; 2.17 (4) and the further references)

The basic descriptions occur in Lev. xxiii.9ff.

'The Lord spoke to Moses and said, Speak to the Israelites in these words: These are the appointed seasons of the Lord, and you shall proclaim them as sacred assemblies; these are my appointed seasons. On six days work may be done, but every seventh day is a Sabbath of sacred rest, a day of sacred assembly, on which you shall do no work. Wherever you live, it is the Lord's sabbath.

These are the appointed seasons of the Lord, the sacred assemblies which you shall proclaim in their appointed order. [5] In the first month on the fourteenth day between dusk and dark is the Lord's Passover. On the fifteenth day of this month begins the Lord's pilgrim-feast of Unleavened Bread; for seven days you shall eat unleavened cakes. On the first day there shall be a sacred assembly; you shall not do your daily work. For seven days you shall present your food-offerings to the Lord. On the seventh day also there shall be a sacred assembly; you shall not do your daily work. The Lord spoke to Moses and said, Speak to the Israelites in these words: When you enter the land which I give you, and you reap its harvest, you shall bring the first sheaf of your harvest to the priest. [11] He shall present the sheaf as a special gift before the Lord on the day after the Sabbath, so as to gain acceptance for yourselves. On the day you present the sheaf, you shall prepare a perfect yearling ram for a whole-offering to the Lord, with the proper grain-offering, two tenths of an *ephah* of flour mixed with oil, as a food-offering to the Lord, of soothing odour, and also with the proper drink-offering, a quarter of a *hin* of wine. You shall eat neither bread, nor grain, parched or fully ripened, during that day, the day on which you bring your God his offering; this is a rule binding on your descendants for all time wherever you live.

[15] From the day after the Sabbath, the day on which you bring your sheaf as a special gift, you shall count seven full weeks. [16] The day after the seventh Sabbath will make fifty days, and then you shall present to the Lord a grain-offering from the new crop. You shall bring from your homes two loaves as a special gift; they shall contain two-tenths of an *ephah* of flour and shall be baked with leaven. They are the Lord's first-fruits. In addition to the bread you

shall present seven perfect yearling sheep, one young bull, and two rams. They shall be a whole-offering to the Lord with the proper grain-offering and the proper drink-offering, a food-offering of soothing odour to the Lord. You shall also prepare one he-goat for a sin-offering and two yearling sheep for a shared-offering, and the priest shall present them in addition to the bread of the first-fruits as a special gift before the Lord. They shall be a holy-gift to the Lord for the priest. On that same day you shall proclaim a sacred assembly for yourselves; you shall not do your daily work. This is a rule binding on your descendants for all time wherever you live.'

Two controversies emerged, in relation to the *ʿomer* and the feast of Shabuot, both of which were caused by an uncertainty over the meaning of 'Sabbath' in vss. 11 and 16. The Boethusians took the word literally and maintained that the *ʿomer* is always to be cut on the day after the *weekly* Sabbath. This means that the cutting of the *ʿomer* invariably took place on the same day of the week, the day after the Sabbath, and that consequently the feast of Shabuot was also bound to take place on the same day of the week, since it followed exactly seven weeks later. Their opponents, however, understood 'Sabbath' to mean 'festival', and hence in this case, the first day of Passover, which is governed by date (Lev. xxiii.5), not by day. From their point of view, the cutting of the *ʿomer* and the feast of Shabuot might take place on other days of the week, *including* the weekly Sabbath, but always on the same dates.

The second controversy concerned the cutting of the *ʿomer* itself. The fact that the Boethusians rejected the cutting of the *ʿomer* on the Sabbath was not simply out of respect for the Sabbath: to cut the *ʿomer* on the Sabbath would give it a resemblance to the sacrificial cult which the priests performed, and which was allowed to take place on the Sabbath. The phrase *bʿsq gdwl* in M.Men. x.3 (2.29) suggests that this was what was intended, and that the ceremony was emphasised precisely because laymen could participate.

So far as *ʿomer* and Shabuot are concerned, Finkelstein suggested that behind the ostensible reason (the meaning of 'Sabbath') lay one issue for the Ḥakamim, another for the Boethusians. For the Ḥakamim, Shabuot was increasingly becoming a celebration of the giving of revelation, hence it was tied, not to the agricultural season, but to the saving history which followed Passover. For the Boethusians, however, the fixed day of the week was important because it simplified the rota of priestly duties and succession in the Temple, and it tied a feast which might be little observed (with a consequent loss of priestly emoluments) in mid-week to a time when it could more easily be observed.

2 The lighting of incense on the Day of Atonement (2.11 and the further references)

The issue here was whether the high priest, on the Day of Atonement, should light the incense outside the Holy of Holies and then enter, or should carry the materials for kindling it inside and only then light it. The Sadducees maintained the former, the Ḥakamim the latter. From the point of view of the priests (especially of the high priest who had to officiate), the Ḥakamic interpretation was fraught with both theological and practical danger. According to Lev. xvi.1ff. (cf. also vss. 12f.), Moses was instructed by Yahweh:

> 'The Lord spoke to Moses after the death of Aaron's two sons, who died when they offered illicit fire before the Lord. He said to him: "Tell your brother Aaron that he must not enter the sanctuary within the Veil, in front of the cover over the Ark, except at the appointed time, on pain of death; for I appear in the cloud above the cover." '

According to the Sadducees, the incense *must* be kindled outside the Holy of Holies if the cloud is to appear above the cover. The penalties attached to Aaron's sons for improper observance are explicit; but even apart from those penalties, the Ḥakamic interpretation involved practical dangers as well. As Finkelstein put it:

> 'According to the Pharisaic norm, the High Priest had to take a censer of coals from the altar in one hand, and a spoon of incense in the other. Holding them before him, he had to walk through the Temple hall into the dark Innermost shrine. There, guided only by the glow of the coals in the censer, his hands burdened, he had to grope to the rock on which the offering was to be made. He placed the censer upon the rock, and poured the incense over the coals in the censer. The Law required this part of the ritual to be performed with his hands rather than with the spoon. To put the incense into

the palms of his hands, he might place the spoon handle in his mouth, between his teeth, so that the incense poured into his palms. Or he might put the handle between his fingers in such a way that the contents could be dropped into his palms. Having achieved this feat he transferred the incense directly from his hands onto the flaming censer. Dressed in highly inflammable linen garments, the High Priest performing this service was in great peril. A spark from the burning incense might readily set his linen clothes afire.' (Finkelstein, *The Pharisees*, p. 657)

The Sadducees relied on a literal understanding of the words 'above the cover': how could the cloud so appear unless the incense were kindled outside? But the Ḥakamim relied on the direct description of Lev. xvi.12:

'He shall take a firepan full of glowing embers from the altar before the Lord, and two handfuls of powdered fragrant incense, and bring them within the Veil.'

But they then had to account for vs.13, and explain how the cloud could appear above:

'He shall put the incense on the fire before the Lord, and the cloud of incense will hide the cover over the Tokens so that he shall not die.'

The record of controversies over the Day of Atonement have an incidental importance, in the sense that they reveal the power of the Ḥakamim to influence the actual procedure of the Temple cult. However exaggerated or stylised the stories may have become, there are no grounds for rejecting the general conclusion to which they point, that the high priest had to accept, at least on some occasions, the Ḥakamic interpretation of Torah. This by no means implies capitulation on *all* points, but simply on points where the meaning of Torah, even on Sadducaic procedures of exegesis, is, as a matter of fact, uncertain, particularly where traditional procedures were well-established. The adjuration, the scriptural readings, and the actual detail of the ceremony all point in this direction, to the reality of a situation in which the Sadducees followed the Ḥakamic (i.e., traditional) procedure and there is thus no reason at all to dismiss the details as 'wishful thinking' on the part of later rabbis, who were trying to portray 'what should have been the case'. The same general conclusion is further supported by other issues in which Ḥakamim quite clearly dominated the situation, as most obviously, for example, in the insistence on a *tebul yom* status for the officiant at the burning of the Red Heifer (see pp. 60–2).

It is possible that the Sadducees were involved in another controversy to do with the Day of Atonement, the drawing of lots, as in B.Yom. 40b; however, as a result of the censored text, it is uncertain whether the Sadducees were, in the original, the controversialists.

3 The kindling of sabbath lights (2.7)

There is no specific information that the Sadducees were the controversialists in this case. Geiger argued that they were (*Nachgelassene Schriften*, III, 287ff.), but it remains speculative. It is, nevertheless, a good example of a permissive use of scriptural silence. Ex. xxv.3 records the strong command, 'You are not even to light your fire at home on the Sabbath day.' It does not, however, say that one must not light a fire on the *eve* of the Sabbath, which can then be kept going. The assertion of this very necessary permission gradually developed into the formal ceremony in the home of kindling the sabbath lights. There may even have been an attempt to extend the principle to the eve of the Day of Atonement, but with less success, according to the comment in 2.7 (the latter part of which gives an indication of the urgency of the permission; cf. the comment in M.Shab. ii.5).

4 The Red Heifer and *tebul yom* (2.31 and the further references)

The ceremony of the Red Heifer and the purpose of its ashes are described in Num. xix.1ff.

'The Lord spoke to Moses and Aaron and said: This is a law and a statute which the Lord has ordained. Tell the Israelites to bring you a red cow without blemish or defect, which has never borne the yoke. You shall give it to Eleazar the priest, and it shall be taken outside the camp and slaughtered to the east of it. Eleazar the priest shall take some of the blood on his finger and sprinkle it seven times towards the front of the Tent of the Presence. The cow shall be burnt in his sight, skin, flesh, and blood, together with the offal. The priest shall then take cedar-wood, marjoram, and scarlet thread, and throw them into the heart of the fire in which the cow is burning. He shall wash his clothes and bathe his body in water; after which he may enter the camp, but he remains ritually unclean till sunset. The man who burnt the cow shall wash his clothes and bathe his body in water, but he also remains unclean till sunset. Then a man who is clean shall collect the ashes of the cow and deposit them outside the camp in a clean place. They shall be reserved for use by the Israelite community in the water of ritual purification; for the cow is a sin-offering. The man who collected the ashes of the cow shall wash his clothes, but he remains unclean till sunset. This rule shall be binding for all time on the Israelites and on the alien who is living with them.

Whoever touches a corpse shall be ritually unclean for seven days. He shall get himself purified with the water of ritual purification on the third day and on the seventh day, and then he shall be clean. If he is not purified both on the third day and on the seventh, he shall not be clean. Everyone who touches a corpse, that is the body of a man who has died, and does not purify himself, defiles the Tabernacle of the Lord. That person shall be cut off from Israel. The water of purification has not been flung over him; he remains unclean, and his impurity is still upon him.'

The issue raised by the Ḥakamim was the degree of holiness, or purity, required of the officiant in the ceremony. According to Lev. xi.27f., 'Whoever touches their dead bodies [i.e., of the animals as defined in vss. 26f.] shall be unclean till evening. Whoever takes up their dead bodies shall wash his clothes but remain unclean till evening. You shall regard them as unclean.' Two other instances of 'uncleanness till evening' (Lev. xv.7, 16) add a specific instruction that the man in question shall bathe in the water and remain unclean till evening; the bathing, therefore, must be taken to apply to the situation in Lev. xi.27. The Sadducees, following what they believed to be the literal intention of the verses, maintained that the person in question remained unclean 'till evening'; only then did the effect of the bathing take place. The Ḥakamim argued that *some* difference must be made by the bathing, even though the full effect did not take place 'till evening'. They, therefore, argued that the person went into a state of 'suspended (or second-grade) uncleanness', and referred to a person in that condition as *tebul yom*. The *tebul yom* was still sufficiently unclean not to be able to enter the Temple beyond the Court of the Gentiles (M.Kel. i.8), hence he certainly could not (if a priest) participate in sacrificial ritual. On the other hand, the *tebul yom* did not communicate uncleanness to others, so that he could continue to participate in the life of the community. Above all, a man in this condition could participate in a sacrificial ritual *outside* the Temple; and since the sacrifice of the Red Heifer took place on the Mount of Olives, the principle of *tebul yom* could most graphically be asserted on that occasion. The Ḥakamim, therefore, went to extreme lengths to ensure that the priest officiating at the ceremony of the Red Heifer was in a condition of being *tebul yom*, which meant first ensuring that he was in a state of impurity in order to be brought into the condition (by bathing) of being *tebul yom*. The vehemence with which they insisted on this can be seen in 3.16. In another incident (T.Par. iii.6) Ishmael b. Phiabi once prepared the Red Heifer in a state of complete purity, the Ḥakamim having failed to make him unclean; they therefore caused the ashes to be scattered and the whole ceremony to be repeated in accordance with their views.

It is clear that although the issue of the Red Heifer was important in its own right, it was the focus of an issue (the status of *tebul yom*) even more vital for those who had ordinary lives to pursue in town and country. The possibilities of contracting uncleanness were so many, that if no condition of suspended uncleanness existed, life would come to a halt, at least for those who were trying to take the observance of Torah seriously. To priests at work in the confines of the Temple, the issue was not so serious – particularly since the application of *tebul yom* did not in any case permit them to continue in the Temple; for that, they would have to wait till sunset.

So far as the Red Heifer itself is concerned, the Ḥakamim went to equally great lengths to ensure the *sanctity* of the ceremony (2.31 (end); 4.11 (end); 4.34 (end)). This in itself resisted any inference that since the *tebul yom* was somehow inferior, the ceremony of the Red Heifer was inferior. On the contrary, the Ḥakamim insisted that a man in a state of *tebul yom* entirely fulfilled the requirements of Num. xix.9, and they surrounded the officiant with extreme precautions against any uncleanness additional to that which brought him to the condition of *tebul yom*. There was thus nothing in the least contradictory in a procedure which took extreme care to eliminate uncleanness and which then led to a formal contamination: such a procedure was indispensable if the principle of *tebul yom* was to be maintained.

The tension of two inter-related principles, of *tebul yom* and of the extreme sanctity of the occasion, may well account for precisely the shift of stringency within the estimate of the *tebul yom* which Finkelstein noticed (II, 661–92, leading to the summary: 'In regard to the *tebul yom*, it is demonstrable that the later trend within Pharisaism was not toward greater leniency for the *tebul yom*, but toward greater severity'). The shift can be seen most clearly in the analogous state of a woman after childbirth, who, according to Lev. xii.2, 5, is in a state of uncleanness for seven days after the birth of a male baby, and for fourteen after the birth of a female baby. In fact, she entered into a suspended state of uncleanness (Sifra 58d) after ritual bathing at the end of this period, and the new condition continued for 33 and 66 days respectively. In this condition, she was 'clean' in all relationships, including those with her husband, but she could not enter the Temple precincts. But the dispute in M.Nidd. x.6 (2.35) between Bet Hillel and Bet Shammai is not simply a matter of greater or lesser stringency between the two schools. The issue *in itself* displays a move towards a higher assessment of the purity of the *tebul yom*.

5 Meal offerings and libations accompanying animal sacrifices (2.28)

In the strict sense, this is not controversial, because only one side of the argument appears, but the possibility of an issue seems clear: according to Lev. vi.16, the remainder of the grain-offering (after the offering of a handful on the altar) was allowed to be eaten by the priests. Did the same ruling apply to grain-offerings which accompanied animal sacrifice? It was clearly in the interests of the priests to argue that it did. But the application of Num. xv.7 and 10 suggested that the whole offering had to be offered on the altar. M.Men. vi.2 (2.28) gives the ruling.

6 Impurity of metals and glass (4.4 and the further references)

This enactment is a good example of the necessity to extend the provisions of Torah to situations not clearly or specifically envisaged in the original text. According to Torah, a dead body imparts uncleanness, not only to human beings, but also to various articles, which in turn can impart uncleanness, as Lev. xi.29–38, for example, makes clear:

'You shall regard these as unclean among creatures that teem on the ground: the mole-rat, the jerboa, and every kind of thorn-tailed lizard; the gecko, the sand-gecko, the wall-gecko, the great lizard, and the chameleon. You shall regard these as unclean among teeming creatures; whoever touches them when they are dead shall be unclean till evening. Anything on which any of them falls when they are dead shall be unclean, any article of wood or garment or skin or sacking, any article in regular use; it shall be plunged into water but shall remain unclean till evening, when it shall be clean. If any of these falls into an earthenware vessel, its contents shall be unclean and it shall be smashed. Any food on which water from such a vessel is poured shall be unclean, and any drink in such a vessel shall be unclean. Anything on which the dead body of such a creature falls shall be unclean; an oven or a stove shall be broken, for they are unclean and you shall treat them as such; but a spring or a cistern where water collects shall remain clean, though whatever touches the dead body shall be unclean. When any of their dead bodies falls on seed intended for sowing, it remains clean; but if the seed has been soaked in water and any dead body falls on it you shall treat it as unclean.'

It will be seen that vessels made of glass or of metal are not included in the list. However, according to B.Shab. 14b (4.4) Jose b. Joezer and Jose b. Joḥanan (the first *zugoth*) extended the provision to vessels of glass, and Simeon b. Shetaḥ (of the next *zugoth*) extended it to metal. (The apparent discrepancy in J.Ket. viii.11 exemplifies the imprecision of names, already noted in the Introduction, but equally it locates the extension firmly in that period.) Although, as B.Shab. 16b (4.5) makes clear, the extension has support in Torah itself, it is equally clear that a development was made in this period, and B.Shab. 16b does not in fact deny it.

7 The right of the daughter of a deceased son to inherit (3.19 and the further references)

The issue over the law of inheritance arose from an attempt to intepret the intentions of Scripture, in defining 'the nearest survivor'. According to Num. xxvii.8, 'When a man dies leaving no son, his patrimony shall pass to his daughter. If he has no daughter, you shall give it to his brothers. If he has no brothers, you shall give it to his father's brothers. If his father had no brothers, then you shall give possession to the nearest survivor in his family, and he shall inherit.'

The *perushim* defended the line of direct descent, so that if a son predeceased his father, the daughter of the son (i.e., the grand-daughter) would inherit from her grandfather when he died: she would, in effect, 'move up' a generation and become as if one of the brothers of the dead man. The Boethusians argued that the *perushim* ought to accept the rights of a daughter (in the first generation) to receive an inheritance, since a daughter must surely be regarded as a nearer survivor than a grand-daughter. The *perushim* rejected the argument. They replied that it does not follow, because the Boethusians themselves admit that the grand-daughter only inherits because she moves up into the place of her father: she does *not* inherit because of her relation to her father as such, but because of her father's relation to his own father (that is, to her grandfather). Thus no rights are established by the relation of daughter to father as such. The force of the reply of the *perushim* is that the grand-daughter does *not* have a claim in her own right, but only because of the connection through the (deceased) son, who was the original heir.

It is possible, as Finkelstein suggested, that the principle was important to the *perushim* who wished to resist the division of small estates into even smaller units. The defence of one major line of descent protected the division of estates among numerous first generation members of a family in which the first heir (the son) had died.

8 False witnesses (2.25 and the further references)

The treatment of false witnesses is described in Dt. xix.16–21:

'When a malicious witness comes forward to give false evidence against a man, and the two disputants stand before the Lord, before the priests and the judges then in office, if, after careful examination by the judges, he be proved to be a false witness giving false evidence against his fellow, you shall treat him as he intended to treat his fellow, and thus rid yourselves of this wickedness. The rest of the people when they hear of it will be afraid: never again will anything as wicked as this be done among you. You shall show no mercy: life for life, eye for eye, tooth for tooth, hand for hand, foot for foot.'

Issue was joined over the point at which the (proven) false witness became liable to punishment. The Sadducees maintained that 'life for life' must be literally understood, and that the false witness only suffered if the falsely accused had suffered. The Ḥakamim, however, argued from vs. 18 that the offence lies in the intention: 'You shall treat him as he *intended* to treat his fellow.'

The Ḥakamic interpretation contradicts Josephus' assertion (1.2; cf. also 7.5) that in matters of punishment the Pharisaioi were more lenient than the Sadducees; furthermore, the point is not simply theoretical, since the Book of Susanna records an execution on the basis of the Ḥakamic principle (that the offence lies in the *intention*, and does not arise from the actual suffering of the victim). There is, of course, one way of interpreting the Ḥakamic principle which would defend the greater leniency of the Pharisaioi, and this is the interpretation recorded in B.Makk. 5b (4.33, beginning). According to that interpretation the emphasis is placed even further on 'intention', and the paradox is produced that only while the *intention* is still in being (and is unfulfilled) can punishment be executed. Hence, if the false witnesses intended to bring about the death of the falsely accused, but he had not been executed before their false witness was proved, the witnesses were executed; but if the falsely accused *had* been executed, their intention was no longer in being, so they were *not* executed. But this would be a curious defence of leniency, and it is in any case unlikely (in view of the story of Susanna and of the dispute between Simeon b. Shetaḥ and Judah b. Tabbai) that it was the originally intended interpretation.

9 The responsibility of the master for damage done by his slave (2.38 (7))

The issue in M.Yad. iv.7, concerning the responsibility of slave-owners for damage done by their slaves, arises from Biblical silence.

The closest Torah comes to discussing the matter is in assessing the responsibility of an owner for damage done by his cattle (as, for example, in Ex. xxi.28). But if an analogy from cattle to humans is not allowed, then Torah is in fact silent on the question of responsibility for slaves. The *perushim* argued that the slaves themselves (since 'they have understanding') are responsible, whereas the Sadducees apparently regarded slaves as a part of their possessions comparable to cattle.

10 Ransom in place of execution

The issue of ransom instead of execution is not strictly controversial, since no record of opposition has survived. It arises from a passage in Sifra, which, according to Finkelstein (II, 700) presupposes 'the existence of judges who would accept ransom to exculpate those condemned to death'. Although speculative, the existence of such judges is likely to have been the case, because the argument in Sifra generalises the requirement in Num. xxxv.32f. (that a *murderer* under sentence of death cannot be ransomed) to *all* cases for which the death penalty is due. Cf. also the controversy over *lex talionis*, pp. 72–4.

11 Water-libations and the beating with the willows at Sukkot (cf. 1.3 and the further references; 3.5 and the further references)

The water-libations and the beating with the willows at the festival of Sukkot (Booths or Tabernacles) constitute one of the most important and interesting of the issues in which a custom not specifically ordered (or in this case even mentioned) in Torah was defended by the Ḥakamim against those who wished to eliminate it. The vehemence with which the customary libations were asserted emerges clearly in the incident(s) in which a high priest who tried to ridicule (or at the least to make inconspicuous) the libation was pelted with the *ethrogim* which were carried in the procession. It seems reasonably clear that the water-libation was connected with Sukkot because Sukkot was originally a festival in which rain for the ensuing year was invoked (see the discussion in Finkelstein, I,

103–13). Only remote hints of this character have survived in Scripture (e.g. Zech. xiv.17), but the vitality of the issue in the period of the second commonwealth (see, e.g., M.R.H. i.2) is a reminder that in discussions of the nature of Sukkot as a New Year Festival in the Biblical period, the continuity of tradition in Israel, as well as the Biblical evidence – or lack of it – must be borne in mind. (K. A. Kitchen, for example, (*Ancient Orient and Old Testament*, London, 1966, pp. 102f.), argued that 'there is no proper (i.e., explicit) evidence in the Old Testament for this (a festival, on a Babylonian model, celebrated at New Year in ancient Israel) at all'; and in a footnote he added: 'Our available evidence shows no New Year aspect for Booths'; while the former statement may be correct, the latter certainly is not, because it adopts a Sadducaic position, that nothing outside Scripture counts as evidence.)

The strength of feeling which the ordinary people – particularly those dependent on the land – held for the traditional form of Sukkot can be seen in their determination to go even beyond the Ḥakamim on one occasion: when the seventh day (the day of the beating of the willow-branches) fell once on the Sabbath, the Boethusians attempted to assert their own (strictly Biblical) interpretation of the feast by putting the willow-branches under heavy stones on the previous evening. Whereas the Ḥakamim strongly supported the people in their assertion of the water-libations, and the beating with the willows (probably because these rites involved the people, not the priests alone), in this case the injunction against bearing burdens on the Sabbath would have inhibited them. Not so the '*amme haAreẓ*, who simply moved the stones. This exemplifies, in miniature, the difference of expectation in the relationship between the people and the Ḥakamim. The Ḥakamim could accept and vigorously uphold customary interpretation, but only in relation to the observance of the whole of Torah; the people were glad to have support for their customs against the strict literalism of the Sadducees or Boethusians, but not at the price of total subservience to the details of Torah, no matter how sympathetically they were interpreted with the needs of the ordinary people in mind.

12 Leniency in punishment (1.2)

M.Makk. i.10 corroborates the endeavour of the Ḥakamim to be lenient, even in capital cases. The Ḥakamim attempted to balance justice with mercy, as, for example, in the famous stories of Abraham; as Finkelstein put it, 'They simply applied the principles of the Torah, whose genius combines normative severity with procedural leniency' (II, 708f.).

13 The equal participation of all Jews in sacrifice: *tamid* and *sheqalim* (4.35 and the further reference; 2.9 and the further reference)

The involvement of all Israel in the Temple became increasingly important as the Diaspora communities grew stronger and more numerous. The feeling for Jerusalem as the 'centre of the world' is widely and diversely attested, as, for example, in the appeals from Egypt to Jerusalem (in Aristeas and the Elephantine papyri), in Philo's emphatic love for Jerusalem (*De Spec. Leg.* i.69f.; *De Prov.* ii.64), or in Hillel's journey to Jerusalem. The Ḥakamim encouraged the involvement of the people in whatever rituals were open to them, and they thus encouraged a real sense of belonging to Jerusalem and the Temple, even at the time when they were also encouraging the dedication of life in holiness to God far away from the Temple; the two were not in the least contradictory. The sense of participation was emphasised in the Ḥakamic insistence on rituals in which the involvement of the people was clear, and it was supremely concentrated in the *sheqalim*, the contribution to the Temple paid by all adult Jews.

The *sheqalim* created a sense of participation because, according to Neh. x.32f.

'we hereby undertake the duty of giving yearly the third of a shekel for the service of the house of our God, for the Bread of the Presence, the regular grain-offering and whole-offering, the Sabbaths, the new moons, the appointed season, the holy-gifts, and the sin-offerings to make expiation on behalf of Israel, and for all else that has to be done in the house of our God.'

The poorer the person, the greater the importance of the principle that the daily sacrifice, *tamid*, should be paid for out of the *sheqalim*, since in that case it was in part 'his' sacrifice. For the priests, it was a matter of sound economy to allow a wealthy person to contribute the daily sacrifice by paying for it himself, if he wished to do so; there is no specific prohibition against this in Torah. The priests, therefore, according to B.Men. 65a (4.35), insisted on a literal understanding of the singular verb in Num. xxviii.4. They were answered, according to the Talmud (which does not specify who gave the answer), by the argument that the lesser was controlled by the greater (the plural) in vs. 2.

There was a further dispute concerning *sheqalim*, whether the priests should be allowed, as they claimed, to exempt themselves from the payment of *sheqalim*. The inverted form of Ben Bukri's opinion in M.Sheq. i.4 (2.9) implies that the priests were accepted as being exempt, but were under no penalty if they wished to contribute. Rn. Joḥanan b. Zakkai reversed the opinion emphatically; and here the issue is clearly the status of priests in Israel (cf. B.Yom. 19a,b, where it is discussed whether priests are messengers of (dependent on) God, or whether they are messengers of (delegated for particular functions by) the people). The Sadducees argued that if the priests contributed *sheqalim*, it would at once convert the daily sacrifices into (at least in part) sacrifices of priests which would then have to be consumed on the altar, instead of being eaten by the priests, as commanded in Lev. vi.23.

14 The stream of *niẓẓoq* (2.38 (7))

The controversy over *niẓẓoq* is complicated by uncertainty over the meaning of the word. Danby's translation follows the main explanation of the commentators, that the question involved is whether a stream of liquid poured from one container to another brings back to the first uncleanness from the second (if it happens to be unclean). According to M.Maksh. v.9, the stream does not convey uncleanness until it reaches a sufficient degree of thickness, as of honey or batter; the Shammaites added a further example. The Sadducees maintained that uncleanness was conveyed by any unbroken stream of water. Once again, the issue was more important for those who were engaged in business or in agricultural work, since the Sadducaic principle would bring life virtually to a standstill. However, the Sadducees were refuted on grounds of internal contradiction, since they did not in fact regard a river as conveying uncleanness, even if it gathered its waters from ground in which bodies had been buried.

15 The washing of hands (2.38; 2.17 and the further references)

The washing of hands is an issue even more complex than most. An aspect of it emerges in M.Yad. iv.6 (2.38), in which the Sadducees ridicule the *perushim* for washing their hands after handling a scroll of Scripture, whereas they do not do so after handling a scroll of a pagan author: the implication is that the scroll of Scripture is unclean, and conveys uncleanness, but the pagan scroll does not. In fact, the *perushim* believed exactly the reverse, that it is no light thing to handle holiness, and that it must be separated from oneself before returning to mundane contact and occupation. This, in itself, is relatively straightforward: what is uncertain is the way in which the dispute is related to the much wider issue of the washing of hands in general, particularly before and after meals. The possibility of hands conveying uncleanness is clearly recognised (as, for example, in M.Yad. iii.2, 2.36), and a basic pattern of hand-washing lies in the attempt to produce a kind of equivalent for non-priests to the practice of priests before certain Temple service and before contact with 'holy things' (i.e., offerings which the priests are to receive) outside the Temple, as Sifre on Num. §116 (6.16) specifically argues. Yet the rabbis were perfectly clear that the custom was recent (i.e., not in Torah), hence their ascription, both of hand-washing and of the practice of *'erub* (see p. 72) to Solomon (4.4). Furthermore, it was a matter of continuing controversy: even as late as the compilation of B.Ḥull. 105a it was not determined how much of the washing of hands was obligatory and how much meritorious; and according to M.Eduy. v.6, 'Eleazar b. Enoch was excommunicated because he threw doubt on the cleanness [or "cleansing", *thrth*] of hands. And when he died the Bet Din sent and set down a stone on his coffin, from which we learn that everyone who is excommunicated and dies while still excommunicated, they stone his coffin.'

This at least suggests the importance of the issue to the Ḥakamic movement, and the reason is not hard to discern: the washing of hands, particularly before and after meals, represented a vital extension or equivalence of Temple action into the community at large – precisely the assertion of equivalence which was established in so many different areas, and which enabled the Ḥakamic interpretation of Judaism to survive the destruction of the Temple with relative ease.

16 *'Erub* (2.6)

The passage (4.4) which attributes the institution of the washing of hands to Solomon also attributes to him the institution of *'erub*. The actual meanings of *'erub* vary slightly, but the intention is the same, to make the proper observance of the Sabbath more possible. The word *'erub* means basically 'merging' or 'mixture', and in this context it refers to a preparation of food sufficient for two meals, and, more particularly, to the consequent merging of households. The *'erub* can be used in different ways: before the Sabbath (or the holy day) begins, the *'erub* may be placed at a particular point which then becomes the centre of a person's abode, so that sabbath limits (*teḥumim*, 2,000 cubits in any direction) are measured from that point; or it may be placed 2,000 cubits from a town boundary, in order to extend the sabbath limits; or it could be placed in a court into which several different houses have access, and in this way the houses could be regarded as a single unit, so that items could be carried from one house to another without infringing the prohibition on the carrying of burdens on the Sabbath. By a slightly different application, a meal prepared before the Sabbath could be left over throughout the Sabbath, so that all cooking done on the Sabbath could then be regarded as a continuation of the work already begun before the Sabbath. There were, of course, various developments, such as the provisional or double *'erub* in M.Erub. iii.5: 'A man may make conditions about his *'erub* and say: "If gentiles come from the east let my *'erub* be to the west, and if from the west, let it be to the east... If a Ḥakam comes from the east let my *'erub* be to the east, and if from the west, let it be to the west..." ' But although the practice of *'erub* extended, until eventually whole towns were included, the principle remained the same, not to evade or weaken sabbath observance, but to make it possible in all circumstances.

The practice of *'erub* was particularly important to those living in humble or crowded conditions, since it gave them the freedom automatically enjoyed by owners of large houses, or of farms, or of estates. For the purposes of sabbath observance, a man's whole property counted as his house, so that he was allowed to carry objects within that area. According to Jer. xvii.21, the offence lay in carrying things in and out of houses – in other words, in continuing daily activity and trade, as Neh. xiii.15 also makes clear. But the smaller the dwelling, the more difficult it became to observe Jeremiah's interpretation, particularly if basic utensils had, for reasons of space, to be left in a court outside. The practice of *'erub* made the observance of the Sabbath as possible for those in small dwellings as for those in large houses.

The fact remains that the practice of *'erub* is not specifically sanctioned in Torah, and M.Erub. vi.2 (2.6) makes it clear that by no means all Jews accepted it. The point of R. Eliezer's opinion in that passage is that the indifference to *'erub* of gentiles who happen to live in the same court as Jews does not destroy the merging of households; their views obviously cannot have substance, because they are in ignorance. But if *Jews* in the same court refuse to participate in *'erub*, then clearly the households are not merged. The discussion certainly envisages a situation in which Jews could be in dispute with each other; and it is not surprising to find in the story immediately following that the dissentient in that particular incident was a Sadducee: *'erub* was exactly the kind of practice to which Sadducees objected, because it had no clear foundation in Torah.

17 *Lex talionis* (7.3; cf. 2.25 and the further references)

The Biblical passage in dispute over the treatment of proven false witnesses (see p. 64) leads to a further question about the interpretation of the *lex talionis* itself: must it always be literally interpreted, or can a payment be offered instead of the exact equivalent? According to the gloss in Meg.Ta'an. (7.3), the Sadducees argued for a literal interpretation, while the *perushim* accepted monetary compensation – except in cases of wilful murder, as B.B.Q. 83b makes clear. Compensation is already envisaged in Josephus *Ant.* iv.280 (8.35): 'He who maims a man shall undergo the like, being deprived of that limb whereof he deprived the other, unless indeed the maimed man be willing to accept money; for the law empowers the victim himself to assess the damage that has befallen him and makes this concession, unless he would show himself too severe.'

In fact the concession is not explicitly allowed in Torah, but it was deduced from two passages. The first is Ex. xxi.12f., 22–5:

'Whoever strikes another man and kills him shall be put to death. But if he did not act with intent, but they met by act of God, the slayer may flee to a place which I will appoint for you. But if a man has the presumption to kill another by treachery, you shall take him even from my altar to be put to death . . . When, in the course of a brawl, a man knocks against a pregnant woman so that she has a miscarriage but suffers no further hurt, then the offender must pay whatever fine the woman's husband demands after assessment. Wherever hurt is done, you shall give life for life, eye for eye, tooth for tooth, hand for hand, foot for foot, burn for burn, bruise for bruise, wound for wound.'

Vss. 12f. establish the principle of wilful murder being punishable only by death. But vss. 22ff. introduce the possibility of monetary compensation in limited circumstances. What has happened in Josephus' interpretation is that the limited possibility has become a wider option on the part of the aggrieved party: he may choose compensation in money if he so desires. This was particularly argued, as in B.B.Q. 83b, from the second passage, Lev. xxiv.17–21.

'When one man strikes another and kills him, he shall be put to death. [18] Whoever strikes a beast and kills it shall make restitution, life for life. When one man injures and disfigures his fellow-countryman, it shall be done to him as he has done; fracture for fracture, eye for eye, tooth for tooth; the injury and disfigurement that he has inflicted upon another shall in turn be inflicted upon him. [21] Whoever strikes a beast and kills it shall make restitution, but whoever strikes a man and kills him shall be put to death.'

Vss. 17 and 21 assert, in the case of animals, *both* the principle of *lex talionis*, *and* compensation. The only way of explaining the discrepancy seemed (to some of the Ḥakamim) to be by drawing a distinction, in the case of human beings, between wilful murder and other killings. But this opinion was not unanimous, even among the rabbis, as two passages in the Mekilta make plain (Nez. viii and x). It may well be, as Finkelstein suggested, that monetary compensation was recognised as legislation in favour of the rich, since they could afford to pay, if necessary, whereas the poor could not evade the *lex talionis*.

18 Manner of execution (2.23 and the further references)

Reference has already been made to this dispute in the Introduction. It is of great importance, since it indicates that in the proliferation of different courts and different jurisdictions, various things were actually being done which the later rabbis regarded as anomalous; note that some of the sources attempted to eliminate the 'anomaly' by a technicality (the testimony of a minor), not by contempt of the court, which suggests that contemporaries of the event were not agreed that it was anomalous. It is also an indication that on some occasions, legal execution was within the competence of the Jews. For a summary of the discussion of the possible connection of this issue with the dispute about resurrection, see A. Guttmann, *Rabbinic Judaism*, p. 138.

19 Impurity of a mother after child-birth

Whether the issue about a mother's purity or impurity after child-birth was an issue specifically with the Sadducees depends primarily on the degree of association between M.Nidd. iv.1 and iv.2 (2.34). If iv.2 is governed by the context in iv.1, then the daughters of the Sadducees are defined in part by an adherence to a stringent interpretation of Lev. xii.1ff.:

> 'When a women conceives and bears a male child, she shall be unclean for seven days, as in the period of her impurity through menstruation. On the eighth day, the child shall have the flesh of his foreskin circumcised. The woman shall wait for thirty-three days because her blood requires purification [lit. 'for thirty-three days she shall continue in the blood of her purity']; she shall touch nothing that is holy, and shall not enter the sanctuary till the days of her purification are completed. If she bears a female child, she shall be unclean for fourteen days as for her menstruation and shall wait for sixty-six days because her blood requires purification.'

The Ḥakamic interpretation took the two periods of waiting as putting the woman in a condition comparable to that of *tebul yom* (see pp. 60ff.): she could not enter the Temple or eat the holy food. But the Samaritans (and by definition, according to M.Nidd. iv.1 and 2 in conjunction, the Sadducees) maintained that the full uncleanness continued. The Ḥakamic interpretation, which allowed of a state of suspended uncleanness, had the effect of permitting, *inter alia*, the resumption of marital intercourse. It depended, partly on identifying the description of the *tebul yom* condition, and also on emphasising that the blood in question is blood of purity, not of impurity.

20 Proof of virginity (7.3)

A further issue of literal interpretation in judicial procedure arose from Dt. xxii.13ff.:

> 'When a man takes a wife and after having intercourse with her turns against her and brings trumped-up charges against her, giving her a bad name and saying, "I took this woman and slept with her and did not find proof of virginity in her", then the girl's father and mother shall take the proof of her virginity to the elders of the town, at the town gate. The girl's father shall say to the elders, "I gave my daughter in marriage to this man, and he has turned against her. He has trumped up a charge and said, 'I have not found proofs of virginity in your daughter.' Here are the proofs." They shall then spread the garment before the elders of the town ...'

According to the gloss in Meg.Ta'an. (7.3), the Sadducees insisted on the literal meaning of the words, and maintained that the stained garment must be produced: 'They shall spread the garment before the elders of the city.' The literal interpretation was also defended by R. Eliezer b. Jacob, according to Sifre on Dt. §237: 'R. Eliezer said: "The words are (to be taken) as they are written."' But this led to the over-severe possibility that the failure to produce the actual evidence meant an automatic assumption of guilt. The rabbis allowed the possibility of other evidence, and also put some onus of proof on the husband, who had to produce evidence that his wife had been unfaithful during the actual period of their betrothal.

21 *Ḥaliẓah* (2.19 and the further reference)

In Dt. xxv.5ff., the principle of levirate marriage is established: if a man dies without leaving a son, his brother (if they have been living together) must marry the widow so that the first born son may perpetuate the dead brother's name. If the brother refuses, the widow can bring him before the elders, at the town gate; if he still refuses, 'she shall pull his sandal off his foot and spit in his face (*bephanaw*) and declare: "Thus we requite the man who will not build up his brother's family." His family shall be known in Israel as the House of the Unsandalled Man.'

How literally should *bephanaw* be taken? According to the gloss in Meg.Ta'an. (7.3), the Sadducees took it literally; but the Ḥakamim understood it in its other, and perfectly legitimate, sense, as 'in front of him'.

22 The immersing of the *menorah* (3.9 and the further reference)

The cause of the controversy over the immersing of the *menorah* (the seven-branched candle-holder of the Temple; for a description, see, e.g., B.Men. 28a–29a) is uncertain, not least since the references to it are so brief. The most likely explanation connects the purifying of the *menorah* with the familiar custom of purifying (at the end of every festival) the Temple vessels in case any non-priest (i.e., pilgrim) had touched them (M.Ḥag. ii.7f). Since the priests alone could touch the *menorah* (see also the discussion in B.Ḥag. 26b), it is not surprising that they mocked the (to them) unnecessary action of the *perushim*. If this explanation is correct, it provides a further illustration of the *perushim* resisting exclusive priestly status.

JOSEPHUS

1.1 Ant. xiii.171–3 (5.9)

'Now at this time there were three schools of thought (*haireseis*) among the Jews, which held different opinions concerning human affairs; the first being that of the Pharisees, the second that of the Sadducees, and the third that of the Essenes. [172] As for the Pharisees, they say that certain events are the work of fate, but not all; as to other events, it depends upon ourselves whether they shall take place or not. The sect of Essenes, however, declares that fate is mistress of all things, and that nothing befalls men unless it be in accordance with her decree. [173] But the Sadducees do away with fate, holding that there is no such thing and that human actions are not achieved in accordance with her decree, but that all things lie within our own power, so that we ourselves are responsible for our well-being, while we suffer misfortune through our own thoughtlessness. Of these matters, however, I have given a more detailed account in the second book of the Jewish History.'

Cf. 1.12 *(11ff.)*; 1.18 *(162ff.)*. *See also* 1.2 *(297f.)*.

1.2 Ant. xiii.288–300 (10.5–7)

As for Hyrcanus, the envy of the Jews was aroused against him by his own successes and those of his sons; particularly hostile to him were the Pharisees, who are one of the Jewish schools, as we have related above. And so great is their influence with the masses that even when they speak against a king or high priest, they immediately gain credence.

[289] Hyrcanus too was a disciple of theirs, and was greatly loved by them. And once he invited them to a feast and entertained them hospitably, and when he saw that they were having a very good time, he began by saying that they knew he wished to be righteous and in everything he did tried to please God and them – for the Pharisees profess such beliefs; [290] at the same time he begged them, if they observed him doing anything wrong or straying from the right path, to lead him back to it and correct him. But they testified to his being

altogether virtuous, and he was delighted with their praise. However, one of the guests, named Eleazar, [291] who had an evil nature and took pleasure in dissension, said, 'Since you have asked to be told the truth, if you wish to be righteous, give up the high priesthood and be content with governing the people.' [292] And when Hyrcanus asked him for what reason he should give up the high priesthood, he replied, 'Because we have heard from our elders that your mother was a captive in the reign of Antiochus Epiphanes.' But the story was false, and Hyrcanus was furious with the man, while all the Pharisees were very indignant.

[293(6)] Then a certain Jonathan, one of Hyrcanus' close friends, belonging to the school of Sadducees, who hold opinions opposed to those of the Pharisees, said that it had been with the general approval of all the Pharisees that Eleazar had made his slanderous statement; and this, he added, would be clear to Hyrcanus if he enquired of them what punishment Eleazar deserved for what he had said. [294] And so Hyrcanus asked the Pharisees what penalty they thought he deserved – for, he said, he would be convinced that the slanderous statement had not been made with their approval if they fixed a penalty commensurate with the crime – and they replied that Eleazar deserved stripes and chains; for they did not think it right to sentence a man to death for calumny, and anyway the Pharisees are naturally lenient in the matter of punishments. [295] At this Hyrcanus became very angry and began to believe that the fellow had slandered him with their approval. And Jonathan in particular inflamed his anger, and so worked upon him [296] that he brought him to join the Sadducaean party and desert the Pharisees, and to abrogate the regulations which they had established for the people, and punish those who observed them. Out of this, of course, grew the hatred of the masses for him and his sons, [297] but of this we shall speak hereafter. For the present I wish merely to explain that the Pharisees had passed on to the people certain regulations handed down by former generations and not recorded in the Laws of Moses, for which reason they are rejected by the Sadducaean group, who hold that only those regulations should be considered valid which were written down (in Scripture), and that those which had been handed down by former generations need not be observed. [298] And concerning these matters the two parties came to have controversies and serious differences, the Sadducees having the confidence of the wealthy alone but no following among the populace, while the Pharisees have the support of the masses. But of these two schools and of the Essenes a detailed account has been given in the second book of my Judaica.

[299(7)] And so Hyrcanus quieted the outbreak, and lived happily thereafter; and when he died after administering the government excellently for thirty-one years, he left five sons. Now he was accounted by God worthy of three of the greatest privileges, the rule of the nation, the office of high priest, and the gift of prophecy; [300] for the Deity was with him and enabled him to foresee and foretell the future; so, for example, he foretold of his two elder sons that they would not remain masters of the state. And the story of their downfall is worth relating, to show how far they were from having their father's good fortune.

> *For references to Hyrcanus, see* 2.4; 2.22 *(*10*);* 3.10; 4.23; 4.25; 7.6. *For descriptions of Pharisees in general, see* 1.1 *and additional references there. On punishments, see* 7.5. *On Joḥanan becoming a Sadducee (*min*), see B.Ber.* 29*a*.

1.3 Ant. xiii.372f. (13.5)

As for Alexander, his own people revolted against him – for the nation was aroused against him – at the celebration of the festival (Sukkot), and as he stood beside the altar and was about to sacrifice, they pelted him with citrons, it being a custom (*nomos*) among the Jews that at the festival of Tabernacles everyone holds wands made of palm branches and citrons – these we have described elsewhere; and they added insult to injury by saying that he was descended from captives and was unfit to hold office and to sacrifice; [373] and being enraged at this, he killed some six thousand of them, and also placed a wooden barrier about the altar and the Temple as far as the coping (of the court) which the priests alone were permitted to enter, and by this means blocked the people's way to him.

> *Cf.* 2.12; 3.6; 4.15; 5.6. *For the palm branches, see* 3.5 *and the further references. Yosippon specifies that the opponents were* prushim: '*At the time of the festival af Sukkot, the king went up to the altar following the pattern of the priests. Then the* prushim, *who are the Ḥakamim, began to pelt him with ethrogim*' (ed. Hominer p. 119, ll. 25ff.).

1.4 Ant. xiii.399–411 (15.5–16.2)

And when the queen saw that he was on the point of death and no longer held to any hope of recovery, she wept and beat her breast, lamenting the bereavement that was about to befall her and her children, and said to him, 'To whom are you thus leaving me and your children, who are in need of help from others, especially when you know how hostile the nation feels toward you?' [400] Thereupon he advised her to follow his suggestions for keeping the throne secure for herself and her children and to conceal his death from the soldiers until she had captured the fortress. [401] And then, he said, on her return to Jerusalem as from a splendid victory, she should yield a certain amount of power to the Pharisees, for if they praised her in return for this sign of regard, they would dispose the nation favourably toward her. These men, he assured her, had so much influence with their fellow-Jews that they could injure those whom they hated and help those to whom they were friendly; [402] for they had the complete confidence of the masses when they spoke harshly of any person, even when they did so out of envy; and he himself, he added, had come into conflict with the nation because these men had been badly treated by him. [403] 'And so', he said, 'when you come to Jerusalem, send for their partisans, and showing them my dead body, permit them, with every sign of sincerity, to treat me as they please, whether they wish to dishonour my corpse by leaving it unburied because of the many injuries they have suffered at my hands, or in their anger wish to offer my dead body any other form of indignity. Promise them also that you will not take any action, while you are on the throne, without their consent. [404] If you speak to them in this manner, I shall receive from them a more splendid burial than I should from you; for once they have the power to do so, they will not choose to treat my corpse badly, and at the same time you will reign securely.' With this exhortation to his wife he died, after reigning twenty-seven years, at the age of forty-nine.

[405 (14.1)] Thereupon Alexandra, after capturing the fortress, conferred with the Pharisees as her husband had suggested, and by placing in their hands all that concerned his corpse and the royal power, stilled their anger against Alexander, and made them her well-wishers and friends. [406] And they in turn went to the people and made public speeches in which they recounted the deeds of

Alexander, and said that in him they had lost a just king, and by their eulogies they so greatly moved the people to mourn and lament that they gave him a more splendid burial than had been given any of the kings before him. [407] Now although Alexander had left two sons, Hyrcanus and Aristobulus, he had bequeathed the royal power to Alexandra. Of these sons the one, Hyrcanus, was incompetent to govern and in addition much preferred a quiet life, while the younger, Aristobulus, was a man of action and high spirit. As for the queen herself, she was loved by the masses because she was thought to disapprove of the crimes committed by her husband.

[408 (2)] Alexandra then appointed Hyrcanus as high priest because of his greater age but more especially because of his lack of energy; and she permitted the Pharisees to do as they liked in all matters, and also commanded the people to obey them; and whatever regulations, introduced by the Pharisees in accordance with the tradition of their fathers, had been abolished by her father-in-law Hyrcanus, these she again restored. [409] And so, while she had the title of sovereign, the Pharisees had the power. For example, they recalled exiles, and freed prisoners, and, in a word, in no way differed from absolute rulers. Nevertheless the queen took thought for the welfare of the kingdom and recruited a large force of mercenaries and also made her own force twice as large, with the result that she struck terror into the local rulers round her and received hostages from them. [410] And throughout the entire country there was quiet except for the Pharisees; for they worked upon the feelings of the queen and tried to persuade her to kill those who had urged Alexander to put the eight hundred to death. Later they themselves cut down one of them, named Diogenes, and his death was followed by that of one after the other, [411] until the leading citizens came to the palace.

For the advice of Jannaeus, cf. 4.22 *(end). For Alexandra, cf.* 1.14*; see also* 4.5*;* 6.5*;* 7.8*;* 7.9.

1.5 Ant. xiv.90f. (5.4)

Gabinius brought Hyrcanus to Jerusalem to have charge of the Temple. He also set up five councils (*synhedria*), and divided the nation into as many districts.

1.6 Ant. xiv.158f., 165–76 (9.2–4)

But as he (Antipater) saw that Hyrcanus was dull and sluggish, he appointed his eldest son Phasael governor of Jerusalem and the surrounding region, and entrusted Galilee to his second son Herod, who was still quite young; he was, in fact, only fifteen years old. [159] But his youth in no way hindered him, and being a young man of high spirit, he quickly found an opportunity for showing his prowess. For on learning that Ezekias, a bandit leader, was overrunning the borders of Syria with a large troop, he caught and killed him and many of the bandits with him . . .

[165] Hyrcanus heard of this but gave the matter no thought; on the contrary he was actually pleased. But the chief Jews were in great fear when they saw how powerful and reckless Herod was and how much he desired to be a dictator. And so they came to Hyrcanus and now openly accused Antipater, saying, 'How long will you keep quiet in the face of what is happening? Do you not see that Antipater and his sons have girded themselves with royal power, while you have only the name of king given you?

[166] But do not let these things go unnoticed, nor consider yourself free of danger because you are careless of yourself and the kingdom. For no longer are Antipater and his sons merely your stewards in the government, and do not deceive yourself with the belief that they are; they are openly acknowledged to be masters. [167] Thus Herod, his son, has killed Ezekias and many of his men in violation of our Law, which forbids us to slay a man, even an evildoer, unless he has first been condemned by the Synhedrion to suffer this fate. He, however, has dared to do this without authority from you.'

[168 (4)] Having heard these arguments, Hyrcanus was persuaded. And his anger was further kindled by the mothers of the men who had been murdered by Herod, for every day in the temple they kept begging the king and the people to have Herod brought to judgement in the Synhedrion for what he had done. Being, therefore, moved by these pleas, Hyrcanus summoned Herod to stand trial for the crimes of which he was accused. Accordingly, after he had settled affairs in Galilee as he thought was to his best interests because his father had advised him not to enter the city as a private individual but with the security of a bodyguard, he came with a troop sufficient for the purposes of the journey, and that he might not appear too formidable to Hyrcanus by arriving with a larger body of men and yet not be entirely unarmed and unprotected; and so he went to his trial. [170] However Sextus, the governor of Syria, wrote to urge Hyrcanus to acquit Herod of the charge, and added threats as to what would happen if he disobeyed. The letter from Sextus gave Hyrcanus a pretext for letting Herod go without suffering any harm from the Synhedrion; for he loved him as a son. [171] But when Herod stood in the Synhedrion with his troops, he overawed them all, and no one of those who had denounced him before his arrival dared to accuse him thereafter; instead there was silence and doubt about what was to be done. [172] While they were in this state, someone named Samaias, an upright man and for that reason superior to fear, arose and said, 'Fellow councillors and King, I do not myself know of, nor do I suppose that you can name, anyone who when summoned before you for trial has ever presented such an appearance. For no matter who it was that came before this Synhedrion for trial, he has shown himself humble and has assumed the manner of one who is fearful and seeks mercy from you by letting his hair grow long and wearing a black garment. [173] But this fine fellow Herod, who is accused of murder and has been summoned on no less grave a charge than this, stands here clothed in purple, with the hair of his head carefully arranged and with his soldiers round him, in order to kill us if we condemn him as the law prescribes, and to save himself by outraging justice. [174] But it is not Herod whom I should blame for this or for putting his own interests above the law, but you and the king, for giving him such great licence. Be assured, however, that God is great, and this man, whom you now wish to release for Hyrcanus' sake, will one day punish you and the king as well.' [175] And he was not mistaken in either part of his prediction. For when Herod assumed royal power, he killed Hyrcanus and all the other members of the Synhedrion with the exception of Samaias. [176] Him he held in the greatest honour, both because of his uprightness and because when the city was later besieged by Herod and Sossius, he advised the people to admit Herod, and said that on account of their sins they would not be able to escape him. And of these events we shall speak in the proper place.

Cf. 1.15, *and see also* 4.28. *Note the conflict of names, here and in* 1.7. *For discussion of the identities of Samaias and Pollion (were they Shemaiah and Abtalion or Shammai and Hillel?) see A. Guttmann,* Rabbinic Judaism, *p.* 53; *S. Zeitlin,* The Rise and Fall of the Judaean State, II *(Philadelphia,* 1967*), p.* 104; *L. Feldmann, 'The Identity of Pollio the Pharisee',* J.Q.R. XLIX *(*1958*), pp.* 53–62.

1.7 Ant. xv.2–4 (1.1)

When Herod had got the rule of all Judaea into his hands, he showed special favour to those of the city's population who had been on his side while he was still a commoner, but those who chose the side of his opponents he harried and punished without ceasing for a single day. [3] Especially honoured by him were Pollion the Pharisee and his disciple Samaias, for during the siege of Jerusalem these men had advised the citizens to admit Herod, and for this they now received their reward. [4] This same Pollion had once, when Herod was on trial for his life, reproachfully foretold to Hyrcanus and the judges that if Herod's life were spared, he would (one day) persecute them all. And in time this turned out to be so, for God fulfilled his words.

Note the conflict of names, here and in 1.6 *(*172*ff.).*

1.8 Ant. xv.319–22 (9.3)

Herod's marriage came about in the following way. [320] There lived in Jerusalem a well-known priest named Simon, the son of one Boethus, an Alexandrian, who had a daughter considered to be the most beautiful woman of her time. [321] And since there was much talk about her among the inhabitants of Jerusalem, Herod, as it happened, first became excited by what he heard, and then, on seeing her, was greatly smitten by the girl's loveliness, but he dismissed the thought of abusing his power in order to achieve his full desire, for he suspected with good reason that he would be accused of violence and tyranny, and so he thought it better to take the girl in marriage. [322] And since Simon was, on the one hand, not illustrious enough to become related (to the king) but, on the other hand, too important to be treated with contempt, Herod fulfilled his desire in a rather reasonable way by increasing his and his daughter's prestige and making their position one of greater honour. That is to say, he promptly removed Jesus, the son of Phabes, from the high priesthood and appointed Simon to this office, and contracted marriage with his daughter.

1.9 Ant. xv.368–71 (10.4)

As for the rest of the populace, he (Herod) demanded that they submit to taking an oath of loyalty, and he compelled them to make a sworn declaration that they would maintain a friendly attitude to his rule. [369] Now most of the people yielded to his demand out of complaisance or fear, but those who showed some spirit and objected to compulsion he got rid of by every possible means. [370] He also tried to persuade Pollion the Pharisee and Samaias and most of their disciples to take the oath, but they would not agree to this, and yet they were not punished as were the others who refused, for they were shown consideration on Pollion's account. [371] And those who are called by us Essenes were also excused from this necessity.

For a Pharisaic refusal to take an oath, see 1.10 *(*42*).*

1.10 Ant. xvii.41–6 (2.4–3.1)

There was also a group of Jews priding itself on its adherence to ancestral custom and claiming to observe the laws of which the Deity approves, and by these men, called Pharisees, the women (of the court) were ruled. These men were able to help the king greatly because of their foresight, and yet they were obviously intent upon combating and injuring him. [42] At least when the whole Jewish people affirmed by an oath that it would be loyal to Caesar and to the king's government, these men, over six thousand in number, refused to take this oath, and when the king punished them with a fine, Pheroras' wife paid the fine for them. [43] In return for her friendliness they foretold – for they were believed to have foreknowledge of things through God's appearances to them – that by God's decree Herod's throne would be taken from him, both from himself and his descendants, and the royal power would fall to her and Pheroras and to any children that they might have. [44] These things, which did not remain unknown to Salome, were reported to the king, as was the news that the Pharisees had corrupted some of the people at court. And the king put to death those of the Pharisees who were most to blame and the eunuch Bagoas and a certain Karos, who was outstanding among his contemporaries for his surpassing beauty and was loved by the king. He also killed all those of his household who approved of what the Pharisees said. [45] Now Bagoas had been carried away by their assurance that he would be called the father and benefactor of him who would some day be set over the people with the title of king, for all the power would belong to him and he would give Bagoas the ability to marry and to beget children of his own.

[46 (3.1)] After punishing the Pharisees who had been convicted of these charges, Herod held a council of his friends and made accusations against Pheroras' wife.

Cf. 1.16.

1.11 Ant. xvii.148–54 (6.1f.)

Certain popular figures rose up against him for the following reason. [149 (2)] Judas, the son of Sariphaeus, and Matthias, the son of Margalothus, were most learned of the Jews and unrivalled interpreters of the ancestral laws, and men especially dear to the people because they educated the youth, for all those who made an effort to acquire virtue used to spend time with them day after day.

[150] When these scholars learned that the king's illness could not be cured, they aroused the youth by telling them that they should pull down all the works built by the king in violation of the laws of their fathers and so obtain from the Law the reward of their pious efforts. It was indeed because of his audacity in making these things in disregard of the Law's provisions, they said, that all those misfortunes, with which he had become familiar to a degree uncommon among mankind, had happened to him, in particular his illness. [151] Now Herod had set about doing certain things that were contrary to the Law, and for these he had been reproached by Judas and Matthias and their followers. For the king had erected over the great gate of the Temple, as a votive offering and at great

cost, a great golden eagle, although the Law forbids those who propose to live in accordance with it to think of setting up images or to make dedications of (the likenesses of) any living creatures.

[152] So these scholars ordered (their disciples) to pull the eagle down, saying that even if there should be some danger of their being doomed to death, still to those about to die for the preservation and safeguarding of their father's way of life, the virtue acquired by them in death would seem far more advantageous than the pleasure of living. For by winning eternal fame and glory for themselves they would be praised by those now living and would leave the ever-memorable (example of their) lives to future generations. [153] Moreover, they said, even those who live without danger cannot escape the misfortune (of death), so that those who strive for virtue do well to accept their fate with praise and honour when they depart this life.

[154] For it makes death much easier when we court danger for a noble cause, and at the same time we obtain for our sons and whatever relatives, men or women, survive us the benefit of the glory which is thereby acquired.

Cf. 1.17.

1.12 Ant. xviii.2–17, 23 (1.1–4, 6)

Quirinius visited Judaea, which had been annexed to Syria, in order to make an assessment of the property of the Jews and to liquidate the estate of Archelaus.

[3] Although the Jews were at first shocked to hear of the registration of property, they gradually condescended, yielding to the arguments of the high priest Joazar, the son of Boethus, to go no further in opposition. So those who were convinced by him declared, without shilly-shallying, the value of their property. [4] But a certain Judas, a Gaulanite from a city named Gamala, who had enlisted the aid of Saddok, a Pharisee, threw himself into the cause of rebellion. They said that the assessment carried with it a status amounting to downright slavery, no less, and appealed to the nation to make a bid for independence. [5] They urged that in case of success the Jews would have laid the foundation of prosperity, while if they failed to obtain any such boon, they would win honour and renown for their

lofty aim; and that Heaven would be their zealous helper to no lesser end than the furthering of their enterprise until it succeeded – all the more if with high devotion in their hearts they stood firm and did not shrink from the bloodshed that might be necessary. [6] Since the populace, when they heard their appeals, responded gladly, the plot to strike boldly made serious progress; and so these men sowed the seed of every kind of misery, which so afflicted the nation that words are inadequate. [7] When wars are set afoot that are bound to rage beyond control, and when friends are done away with who might have alleviated the suffering, when raids are made by great hordes of brigands and men of the highest standing are assassinated, it is supposed to be the common welfare that is upheld, but the truth is that in such cases the motive is private gain. [8] They sowed the seed from which sprang strife between factions and the slaughter of fellow citizens. Some were slain in civil strife, for these men madly had recourse to butchery of each other and of themselves from a longing not to be outdone by their opponents; others were slain by the enemy in war. Then came famine, reserved to exhibit the last degree of shamelessness, followed by the storming and razing of cities until at last the very Temple of God was ravaged by the enemy's fire through this revolt. [9] Here is a lesson that an innovation and reform in ancestral traditions weighs heavily in the scale in leading to the destruction of the congregation of the people. In this case certainly, Judas and Saddok started among us an intrusive fourth school of philosophy; and when they had won an abundance of devotees, they filled the body politic immediately with tumult, also planting the seeds of those troubles which subsequently overtook it, all because of the novelty of this hitherto unknown philosophy that I shall now describe. [10] My reason for giving this brief account of it is chiefly that the zeal which Judas and Saddok inspired in the younger element meant the ruin of our cause.

[11 (2)] The Jews, from the most ancient times, had three philosophies pertaining to their traditions, that of the Essenes, that of the Sadducees, and, thirdly, that of the group called the Pharisees. To be sure, I have spoken about them in the second book of the Jewish War, but nevertheless I shall here too dwell on them for a moment.

[12 (3)] The Pharisees simplify their standard of living, making no concession to luxury. They follow the guidance of that which their doctrine has selected and transmitted as good, attaching the chief importance to the observance of those commandments which it has seen fit to dictate to them. They show respect and deference to their elders, nor do they rashly presume to contradict their proposals.

[13] Though they postulate that everything is brought about by fate, still they do not deprive the human will of the pursuit of what is in man's power, since it was God's good pleasure that there should be a fusion and that the will of man with his virtue and vice should be admitted to the council-chamber of fate. [14] They believe that souls have power to survive death and that there are rewards and punishments under the earth for those who have led lives of virtue or vice: eternal imprisonment is the lot of evil souls, while the good souls receive an easy passage to a new life. [15] Because of these views they are, as a matter of fact, extremely influential among the townsfolk; and all prayers and sacred rites of divine worship are performed according to their exposition. This is the great tribute that the inhabitants of the cities, by practising the highest ideals both in their way of living and in their discourse, have paid to the excellence of the Pharisees.

[16 (4)] The Sadducees hold that the soul perishes along with the body. They own no observance of any sort apart from the laws; in fact, they reckon it a virtue to dispute with the teachers of the path of wisdom that they pursue. [17] There are but few men to whom this doctrine has been made known, but these are men of the highest standing. They accomplish practically nothing, however. For whenever they assume some office, though they submit unwillingly and perforce, yet submit they do to the formulas of the Pharisees, since otherwise the masses would not tolerate them . . .

[23 (6)] As for the fourth of the philosophies, Judas the Galilaean set himself up as leader of it. This school agrees in all other respects with the opinions of the Pharisees, except that they have a passion for liberty that is almost unconquerable, since they are convinced that God alone is their leader and master.

For the description of the Pharisees, cf. 1.1 *and further references. On Judas, see* 1.18.

1.13 Ant. xx.264 (12.1)

They (our people) give credit for wisdom to those alone who have an exact knowledge of the Law and who are capable of interpreting the meaning of the Holy Scriptures. Consequently, though many have laboriously undertaken this training, scarcely two or three have succeeded, and have forthwith reaped the fruit of their labours.

1.14 War i.107–14 (5.1–3)

Alexander bequeathed the kingdom to his wife Alexandra, being convinced that the Jews would bow to her authority as they would to no other, because by her utter lack of his brutality and by her opposition to his crimes she had won the affections of the populace. [108] Nor was he mistaken in these expectations; for this frail woman firmly held the reins of government, thanks to her reputation for piety. She was, indeed, the very strictest observer of the national traditions and would deprive of office any offenders against the sacred laws. [109] Of the two sons whom she had by Alexander, she appointed the elder, Hyrcanus, high priest, out of consideration alike for his age and his disposition, which was too lethargic to be troubled about public affairs; the younger, Aristobulus, as a hot-head, she confined to a private life.

[110 (2)] Beside Alexandra, and growing as she grew, arose the Pharisees, a body of Jews with the reputation of excelling the rest of their nation in the observances of religion, and as exact exponents of the laws. [111] To them, being herself intensely religious, she listened with too great deference; while they, gradually taking advantage of an ingenuous woman, became at length the real administrators of the state, at liberty to banish and to recall, to loose and to bind, whom they would. In short, the enjoyments of royal authority were theirs; its expenses and burthens fell to Alexandra. [112] She proved, however, to be a wonderful administrator in larger affairs, and, by continual recruiting, doubled her army, besides collecting a considerable body of foreign troops; so that she not only strengthened her own nation, but became a formidable foe to foreign potentates. But if she ruled the nation, the Pharisees ruled her.

[113 (3)] Thus they put to death Diogenes, a distinguished man who had been a friend of Alexander, accusing him of having advised the king to crucify his eight hundred victims. They further urged Alexandra to make away with the others who had instigated Alexander to punish those men; and as she from superstitious motives always gave way, they proceeded to kill whomsoever they would. [114] The most eminent of the citizens thus imperilled sought refuge with Aristobulus, who persuaded his mother to spare their lives in consideration of their rank, but, if she was not satisfied of their innocence, to expel them from the city. Their security being thus guaranteed, they dispersed about the country.

Cf. 1.4 *and the further references.*

1.15 War i.204–11 (10.5–7)

Herod, energetic by nature, at once found material to test his metal. Discovering that Ezekias, a brigand-chief, at the head of a large horde, was ravaging the district on the Syrian frontier, he caught him and put him and many of the brigands to death. [205] This welcome achievement was immensely admired by the Syrians. Up and down the villages and in the towns the praises of Herod were sung, as the restorer of their peace and possessions. This exploit, moreover, brought him to the notice of Sextus Caesar, a kinsman of the great Caesar and governor of Syria. [206] Phasael, on his side, with a generous emulation, vied with his brother's reputation; he increased his popularity with the inhabitants of Jerusalem, and kept the city under control without any tactless abuse of authority.

[207] Antipater, in consequence, was courted by the nation as if he were king and universally honoured as lord of the realm. Notwithstanding this, his affection for Hyrcanus and his loyalty to him underwent no change.

[208 (6)] But it is impossible in prosperity to escape envy. The young man's fame already caused Hyrcanus a secret pang. He was vexed in particular by Herod's successes and by the arrival of messenger after messenger with news of each new honour that he had won. His resentment was further roused by a number of malicious persons at court, who had taken offence at the prudent behaviour either of Antipater or of his sons. [209] Hyrcanus, they said, had abandoned to Antipater and his sons the direction of affairs, and rested content with the mere title, without the authority, of a king. How long would he be so mistaken as to rear kings to his own undoing? No longer masquerading as viceroys, they had now openly declared themselves masters of the state, thrusting him aside; seeing that, without either oral or written instructions from Hyrcanus, Herod, in violation of Jewish law, had put all this large number of people to death. If he is not king but still a commoner, he ought to appear in court and answer for his conduct to his king and to his country's laws, which do not permit anyone to be put to death without trial.

[210 (7)] These words gradually inflamed Hyrcanus; until at last, in an explosion of rage, he summoned Herod to trial. Herod, on his father's advice, and with the confidence which his own conduct inspired, went up to the capital, after posting garrisons throughout Galilee. He went with a strong escort, calculated to avoid, on the one hand, the appearance of wishing to depose Hyrcanus by bringing an overwhelming force, and, on the other, the risk of falling unprotected a prey to envy. [211] Sextus Caesar, however, fearing that the young man might be isolated by his adversaries and meet with misfortune, sent express orders to Hyrcanus to clear Herod of the charge of manslaughter. Hyrcanus, being inclined to take that course on other grounds, for he loved Herod, acquitted him.

Cf. 1.6.

1.16 War i.571 (29.2)

Herod, accordingly, assembled a council (*synhedrion*) of his friends and relations and accused the wretched woman (Pheroras' wife) of numerous misdeeds, among others of insulting his own daughters, of subsidising the Pharisees to oppress him, and of alienating his brother, after bewitching him with drugs.

Cf. 1.10.

1.17 War i.648–50 (33.2)

There were in the capital two *sophistai* (experts) with a reputation as profound experts in the laws of their country, who consequently enjoyed the highest esteem of the whole nation; their names were Judas, son of Sepphoraeus, and Matthias, son of Margalus. [649] Their lectures on the laws were attended by a large youthful audience, and day after day they drew together quite an army of men in their prime. Hearing now that the king was gradually sinking under despondency and disease, these doctors threw out hints to their friends that this was the fitting moment to avenge God's honour and to pull down those structures which had been erected in defiance of their fathers' laws. [650] It was, in fact, unlawful to place in the Temple either images or busts or any representation whatsoever of a living creature; notwithstanding this, the king had erected over the great gate a golden eagle. This it was which these doctors now exhorted their disciples to cut down, telling them that, even if the action proved hazardous, it was a noble deed to die for the law of one's country; for the souls of those who came to such an end attained immortality and an eternally abiding sense of felicity; it was only the ignoble, uninitiated in their philosophy, who clung in their ignorance to life and preferred death on a sick-bed to that of a hero.

Cf. 1.11.

1.18 War ii.118–19, 162–6 (8.2, 14)

Under the administration of Coponius, a Galilean, named Judas, incited his countrymen to revolt, upbraiding them as cowards for consenting to pay tribute to the Romans and tolerating mortal masters, after having God for their lord. This man was a sophist (*sophistes*) who founded a sect of his own, having nothing in common with the others.

[119 (2)] Jewish philosophy, in fact, takes three forms. The followers of the first school are called Pharisees, of the second Sadducees, of the third Essenes . . .

[162 (14)] Of the two first-named schools, the Pharisees, who are considered the most accurate interpreters of the Laws, and hold the position of the leading sect, attribute everything to fate and to God; [163] they hold that to act rightly or otherwise rests, indeed, for the most part with men, but that in each action fate co-operates. Every soul, they maintain, is imperishable, but the soul of the good alone passes into another body, while the souls of the wicked suffer eternal punishment.

[164] The Sadducees, the second of the orders, do away with fate

altogether, and remove God beyond, not merely the commission, but the very sight, of evil. [165] They maintain that man has the free choice of good or evil, and that it rests with each man's will whether he follows the one or the other. As for the persistence of the soul after death, penalties in the underworld, and rewards, they will have none of them.

[166] The Pharisees are affectionate to each other and cultivate harmonious relations with the community. The Sadducees, on the contrary, are, even among themselves, rather boorish in their behaviour, and in their intercourse with their peers are as rude as to aliens. Such is what I have to say on the Jewish philosophical schools.

For the description of the Pharisees, cf. 1.1 *and the further references. On Judas, see* 1.12.

1.19 War ii.411–17 (17.3)

Thereupon the principal citizens assembled with the chief priests and the most notable Pharisees to deliberate on the position of affairs, now that they were faced with what seemed irreparable disaster. Deciding to try the effect of an appeal to the revolutionaries, they called the people together before the bronze gate – that of the inner Temple facing eastward. [412] They began by expressing the keenest indignation at the audacity of this revolt and at their country being thus threatened with so serious a war. They then proceeded to expose the absurdity of the alleged pretext. Their forefathers, they said, had adorned the sanctuary mainly at the expense of aliens and had always accepted the gifts of foreign nations; [413] not only had they never taken the sacrilegious step of forbidding anyone to offer sacrifice, but they had set up around the Temple the dedicatory offerings which were still to be seen and had remained there for so long a time. [414] But now here were these men, who were provoking the arms of the Romans and courting a war with them, introducing a strange innovation into their religion, and, besides endangering the city, laying it open to the charge of impiety, if Jews henceforth were to be the only people to allow no alien the right of sacrifice or worship. [415] Should such a law be introduced in the case of any private individual, they would be indignant at so inhumane a decree;

yet they made light of putting the Romans and Caesar outside the pale. [416] It was to be feared, however, that, once they rejected the sacrifices for the Romans, they might not be allowed to offer sacrifice even for themselves, and that their city would be placed outside the pale of the empire, unless, with a speedy return to discretion, they restored the sacrifices and made amends for the insult before the report reached the ears of those whom they had insulted.

[417 (4)] In the course of these remonstrances they produced priestly experts on the traditions, who declared that all their ancestors had accepted the sacrifices of aliens. But not one of the revolutionary party would listen to them; even the Temple ministers failed to come to their support and were thus instrumental in bringing about the war.

1.20 War iv.147–61 (3.6–9)

In the end, to such abject prostration and terror were the people reduced and to such heights of madness rose these brigands, that they actually took upon themselves the election to the high priesthood. [148] Abrogating the claims of those families from which in turn the high priests had always been drawn, they appointed to that office ignoble and low born individuals, in order to gain accomplices in their impious crimes; [149] for persons who had undeservedly attained to the highest dignity were bound to obey those who had conferred it. [150] Moreover, by various devices and libellous statements, they brought the official authorities into collision with each other, finding their own opportunity in the bickerings of those who should have kept them in check; until, glutted with the wrongs which they had done to men, they transferred their insolence to the Deity and with polluted feet invaded the sanctuary.

[151 (7)] An insurrection of the populace was at length pending, instigated by Ananus, the senior of the chief priests, a man of profound sanity, who might possibly have saved the city, had he escaped the conspirators' hands. At this threat these wretches converted the Temple of God into their fortress and refuge from any outbreak of popular violence, and made the Holy Place the headquarters of their tyranny. [152] To these horrors was added a spice of mockery more galling than their actions. For, to test the abject submission of the populace and make trial of their own strength, they essayed to appoint the high priests by lot, although, as we have stated, the succession was hereditary. [154] As pretext for this scheme they adduced ancient custom, asserting that in old days the high priesthood had been determined by lot; but in reality their action was the abrogation of established practice and a trick to make themselves supreme by getting these appointments into their own hands.

[155 (8)] They accordingly summoned one of the high-priestly clans, called Eniachin, and cast lots for a high priest. By chance the lot fell to one who proved a signal illustration of their depravity; he was an individual named Phanni, son of Samuel, of the village of Aphthia, a man who not only was not descended from high priests, but was such a clown that he scarcely knew what the high priesthood meant. [156] At any rate they dragged their reluctant victim out of the country and, dressing him up for his assumed part, as on the stage, put the sacred vestments upon him and instructed him how to act in keeping with the occasion. [157] To them this monstrous impiety was a subject for jesting and sport, but the other priests, beholding from a distance this mockery of their Law, could not restrain their tears and bemoaned the degradation of the sacred honours.

[158 (9)] This latest outrage was more than the people could stand, and as if for the overthrow of a despotism one and all were now roused. [159] For their leaders of outstanding reputation, such as Gorion, son of Joseph, and Symeon, son of Gamaliel, by public addresses to the whole assembly and by private visits to individuals, urged them to delay no longer to punish these wreckers of liberty and purge the sanctuary of its bloodstained polluters. [160] Their efforts were supported by the most eminent of the high priests, Jesus, son of Gamalas, and Ananus, son of Ananus, who at their meetings vehemently upbraided the people for their apathy and incited them against the Zealots; [161] for so these miscreants called themselves, as though they were zealous in the cause of virtue and not for vice in its basest and most extravagant form.

1.21 Cont.Ap. i.42 (9)

We have given practical proof of how we approach our own Scriptures. For, although such long ages have now passed, no one has ventured either to add, or to remove, or to alter a single syllable; and it is an instinct with every Jew, from the day of his birth, to regard them as the decrees of God, to abide by them, and, if need be, cheerfully to die for them.

1.22 Life 10–12 (2)

At about the age of sixteen I determined to gain personal experience of the sects among us. These, as I have frequently mentioned, are three in number – the first that of the Pharisees, the second that of the Sadducees, and the third that of the Essenes. I thought that, after a thorough investigation, I should be in a position to select the best.

[11] So I submitted myself to hard training and laborious exercises and passed through the three courses. Not content, however, with the experience thus gained, on hearing of one named Bannus, who dwelt in the wilderness, wearing only such clothing as trees provided, feeding on such things as grew of themselves, and using frequent ablutions of cold water, by day and night, for purity's sake, I became his devoted disciple. [12] With him I lived for three years and, having accomplished my purpose, returned to the city. Being now in my nineteenth year I began to govern my life by the rule of the Pharisees, a sect having points of resemblance to that which the Greeks call the Stoic school.

1.23 Life 21 (5)

When Menahem and the chieftains of the band of brigands had been put to death I ventured out of the Temple and once more consorted with the chief priests and the leading (*protoi*) Pharisees.

1.24 Life 189–98 (38f.)

Meanwhile, the hatred borne me by John, son of Levi, who was aggrieved at my success, was growing more intense, and he determined at all costs to have me removed. Accordingly, after fortifying his native town of Gischala, [190] he dispatched his brother Simon and Jonathan, son of Sisenna, with about a hundred armed men, to Jerusalem, to Simon, son of Gamaliel, to entreat him to induce the national assembly of Jerusalem to deprive me of the command of

Galilee and to vote for his appointment to the post. [191] This Simon was a native of Jerusalem, of a very illustrious family, and of the sect of the Pharisees, who have the reputation of being unrivalled experts in their country's laws. [192] A man highly gifted with intelligence and judgement, he could by sheer genius retrieve an unfortunate situation in affairs of state. He was John's old and intimate friend, and, at the time, was at variance with me. [193] On receiving this application he exerted himself to persuade the high priests Ananus and Jesus, son of Gamalas, and some others of their party to clip my sprouting wings and not suffer me to mount to the pinnacle of fame. He observed that my removal from Galilee would be to their advantage, and urged them to act without delay, for fear that I should get wind of their plans and march with a large army upon Jerusalem. [194] Such was Simon's advice. In reply, Ananus, the high priest, represented the difficulties of the action suggested, in view of the testimonials from many of the chief priests and leaders of the people to my capacity as a general; adding that to accuse a man against whom no just charge could be brought was a dishonourable proceeding.

[195 (39)] On hearing this speech of Ananus, Simon implored the embassy to keep to themselves and not divulge what had passed at the conference; asserting that he would see to it that I was speedily superseded in Galilee. Then calling up John's brother he instructed him to send presents to Ananus and his friends, as a likely method of inducing them to change their minds. [196] Indeed Simon eventually achieved his purpose; for, as the result of bribery, Ananus and his party agreed to expel me from Galilee, while every one else in the city remained ignorant of the plot. The scheme agreed upon was to send a deputation comprising persons of different classes of society but of equal standing in education. [197] Two of them, Jonathan and Ananias, were from the lower ranks and adherents of the Pharisees; the third, Jozar, also a Pharisee, came of a priestly family; the youngest, Simon, was descended from high priests. [198] Their instructions were to approach the Galileans and ascertain the reason for their devotion to me. If they attributed it to my being a native of Jerusalem, they were to reply that so were all four of them; if to my expert knowledge of their laws, they should retort that neither were they ignorant of the customs of their fathers; if, again, they asserted that their affection was due to my priestly office, they should answer that two of them were likewise priests.

MISHNAH

2.1 Ber. ix.5

At the close of every Blessing in the Temple they used to say, 'For everlasting'; but after the *minim* [var. 'Sadducees'] had taught corruptly and said that there is no world except one, it was ordained that they should say, 'From everlasting to everlasting'.

2.2 Dem. ii.2f.

He who accepts on himself to be trustworthy (*ne'eman*), tithes what he eats and what he sells and what he buys, and does not stay as a guest with an *'am haAreẓ*. R. Judah says: 'Even if he stays with an *'am haAreẓ*, he is *ne'eman*.' They said to him: 'If he is not trustworthy in respect to himself, will he be in respect to others?'

He who accepts on himself to be a *ḥaber* may not sell to an *'am haAreẓ* anything wet or dry, or buy anything wet. He may not be the guest of an *'am haAreẓ*, nor may he receive him as a guest in his own clothes. R. Judah said: 'Nor may he rear small animals or be profuse in vows or levity or contract uncleanness from the dead, but should minister in the *bet haMidrash*.' They said to him: 'These things do not come under the general principle (*kelal*).'

For general descriptions of the ḥaberim, *see* 3.2*;* 4.36*;* 5.5. *On contact with an* 'am haAreẓ, *see* 3.12*;* 4.3. *For other references to* ḥaber/ḥaburah, *see the Index.*

2.3 Shebi. x.3,4

(A loan governed by) *prozbul* is not cancelled (in the seventh year of Release). This is one of the things Hillel the Elder enacted. When he saw that people hesitated to lend to each other and transgressed what is written, 'See that you do not harbour iniquitous thoughts . . .' [Dt. xv.9], Hillel ordained the *prozbul*.

This is the form of the *prozbul*: 'I affirm [or lit. 'hand over'] to you, n., and n., the judges in n., that in the case of debts due to me,

I will collect whenever I will.' And the judges or the witnesses sign below.

2.4 M.Sh. v.15

Joḥanan the high priest did away with the avowal concerning the tithe. He made an end also of the 'Awakeners' (*m'wrrin*) and the 'Stunners' (*nwqphin*). Until his days the hammer used to smite in Jerusalem. And in his days none needed to enquire concerning *demai*-produce.

Cf. 1.2 *and the further references.*

2.5 Shab. i.4

These are among the *halakoth* which they spoke in the upper room of Ḥananiah b. Ḥezekiah b. Gorion when they went up to see him. They voted and Bet Shammai outnumbered Bet Hillel; and they enacted eighteen things on that day.

An interpretation of the eighteen enactments is given in J.Shab. i.4–9.

2.6 Erub. vi.1f.

If a man lived in the same courtyard with a gentile or with one that does not admit *'erub*, this restricts him. [Some MSS 'so according to R. Meir'.] R. Eliezer b. Jacob says: 'He can never suffer restriction unless it is two Israelites who restrict each other.'

Rn. Gamaliel said: 'It happened once that a certain Sadducee lived with us in the same court in Jerusalem, and my father said to us, "Hurry and put out all the vessels in the alley before he brings out his and so restricts you." ' R. Judah records it in another way (*blshwn aḥr*): 'Hurry and do what is needful in the alley, before (the eve of Sabbath) is ended and he so restricts you.'

For the connection of Solomon with 'erub, *see* 4.4.

2.7 Pes. iv.4

Where the custom (*nhg*) is to eat flesh roast on the nights of Passover, they may eat it so; where it is not the custom they may not do so. Where the custom is to kindle the lamp on the nights of the Day of Atonement, they may do so; where the custom is not to kindle it, they may not do so. But they may kindle it in synagogues, houses of study, dark alleys and over sick persons.

2.8 Pes. v.8

As the rite was performed on a weekday, so it was performed on a Sabbath, except that the priests swilled the Temple fore-court, which was not with the consent of the Ḥakamim (*shlo brẓwn ḥkmim*). R. Judah says: 'One (of the priests) used to fill a cup from the mingled blood and sprinkle it in one action against the sides of the altar (to validate any offering in which the blood had been wrongly treated).' But the Ḥakamim did not agree with him (*wlo hwdw lw ḥkmim*).

2.9 Sheq. i.3,4

On the fifteenth of Adar, the tables (of the money-changers) were set up in the city [*mdinah*, perhaps 'provinces'], and on the twenty-fifth, they set them up in the Temple. After they were set up, they began to accept pledges (from those who had not yet paid the Shekel dues). From whom did they accept pledges? From Levites, Israelites, proselytes, and freed slaves, but not from women, slaves or minors. If the father had begun to pay the Shekel on behalf of a minor, he may never again cease to pay it. They did not accept pledges from the priests, in the interests of peace (*mphney drkey shlwm*).

R. Judah said: 'Ben Bukri testified in Yavneh that any priest who contributed the Shekel was not guilty of sin.' Rn. Joḥanan b. Zakkai said to him: 'Not so: any priest who does *not* contribute the Shekel is guilty of sin.' But the priests interpret (*dwrshim*) Scripture to their own advantage: 'Every grain-offering of a priest shall be a complete offering (wholly burnt); it shall not be eaten' (Lev. vi.23): since the '*omer*, the two loaves, and the shewbread are ours (and are paid for out of the Shekalim), how can they be eaten (if we contribute to them – they must be burnt)?'

See also 2.10.

2.10 Sheq. iii.3

Those belonging to the house of Rn. Gamaliel used to go in with their Shekel between their fingers and throw it in front of the one who was to receive the offering [i.e., accept *terumah*], and he who received *terumah* deliberately thrust it into the basket. He who received *terumah* never took it up without saying, 'Shall I take it up?', and they thrice made answer, 'Take up *terumah*! take up *terumah*! take up *terumah*!'

See also 2.9.

2.11 Yom. i.5f.

The elders of the court (*zqney bet din*) delivered him (the high priest on the eve of the Day of Atonement) to the elders of the priesthood (*zqney khwnah*) and they brought him up to the upper chamber of the House of Abtinas. They adjured him and took their leave and went away having said to him, 'My Lord High Priest, we are delegates (*shlwḥin*) of the Court, and you are our delegate and the delegate of the Court. We adjure you by him who made his name to dwell in this house that you change nothing of what we have said to you.' He turned aside (√*prsh*) and wept and they turned aside (√*prsh*) and wept.

If he was a Ḥakam he used to expound (Scripture), and if not, the disciples of the Ḥakamim (*tlmidey ḥkmim*) used to expound before him . . .

Cf. 3.4; 4.12; 4.13; 5.8.

2.12 Sukk. iv.9

To the one pouring out (*lmnsk*) they say, 'Lift up your hand!' For once a certain one (*aḥd*) poured it over his feet, and all the people pelted him with their *ethrogim*.

Cf. 1.3 *and the further references.*

2.13 Sukk. v.4

Ḥasidim and men of works (*anshe ma'aseh*) used to dance before them with burning torches in their hands, singing songs and praises . . .

2.14 R.H. ii.1f.

If the witness (to the first appearance of the new moon) was not known, another was sent with him to testify of him. At first they used to admit evidence about the new moon from any man, but after the evil doings of the heretics (*haMinim*) they enacted that evidence should be admitted only from those whom they knew.

At first they used to kindle flares (to spread the news of the new moon), but after the evil doings of the Samaritans (*kuthim*) they enacted that messengers should go forth.

Cf. 3.7; 4.17; 5.10.

2.15 Ḥag. i.8

(The rules about) release from vows float in the air and have nothing to support them. The rules about the Sabbath, festival offerings, and sacrilege [misappropriation of consecrated property] are as mountains hanging by a hair, for Scripture is slight, but the rules many.

2.16 Ḥag. ii.2

Jose ben Joezer says: 'One may not perform *semikah*.' Jose b. Joḥanan says, 'He may.' Joshua b. Peraḥiah says, 'He may not.'

Nittai the Arbelite says, 'He may.' Judah b. Tabbai says, 'He may not.' Simeon b. Shetaḥ says, 'He may.' Shemaiah says, 'He may.' Abtalion says, 'He may not.' Hillel and Menaḥem did not disagree. Menaḥem went out and Shammai came in. Shammai says, 'He may not perform *semikah*.' Hillel says, 'He may.' The first (of each) were *nasi* (*nsi'im*) the second *ab* (*aboth*) *bet din*.

Cf. 3.8; 4.18. *On* semikah, *see the discussion in Guttmann,* Rabbinic Judaism, *pp.* 35*ff*.

2.17 Ḥag. ii.4f.

If the feast of Weeks (Pentecost) fell on the eve of a Sabbath, the school of Shammai say: 'The day for slaughtering is after the Sabbath.' And the school of Hillel say: 'It needs no other day for slaughtering.' But they agree that if (the feast) fell on a Sabbath, the day for slaughtering is after the Sabbath. The high priest may not put on his high-priestly vestments, and mourning and fasting are permitted, to lend no support to the words of those who say, 'The feast of Weeks falls on the day after the Sabbath.'

[5] Before touching unconsecrated food or (Second) Tithe or Heave-offering, the hands need to be washed simply [as governed by M.Yad. i.1]. For Hallowed Things, they need to be immersed; and in what concerns the Sin-offering water, if a man's hands are unclean, his whole body is reckoned unclean.

For the feast of Weeks, cf. 4.35 *(end)*; 7.2; 2.29. *On the washing of hands, cf.* 4.1; 4.2; 4.4; 6.16.

2.18 Ḥag. ii.7

For *prushim* the clothes of an *'am haAreẓ* count as suffering contact -(*midras-*) uncleanness; for those who eat of the priest's due (*terumah*) the clothes of *prushim* count as suffering *midras*-uncleanness; for those who eat of Hallowed Things (*qwdsh*) the clothes of those who eat of the priest's due (Heave-offering) count as suffering *midras*-uncleanness; for those who occupy themselves with the Sin-offering water the clothes of those who eat of Hallowed Things count as suffering *midras*-uncleanness. Joseph b. Joezer was the most pious (*ḥasid*) of the priesthood, yet for those who ate of hallowed things his cloth counted as suffering *midras*-uncleanness. Joḥanan b. Gudgada used to eat according to the cleanness of Hallowed Things all his days, yet for those who occupied themselves with the Sin-offering water, his cloth counted as suffering *midras*-uncleanness.

2.19 Yeb. xii.6

This is the prescribed rite of *ḥaliẓah* [Dt. xxv.7–10]. When the man and his deceased brother's wife are come to the court the judges offer such advice to the man as befits him, for it is written, 'Then the elders of the town shall summon him and reason with him.' And she shall say: 'My husband's brother refuses to perpetuate his brother's name in Israel: he will not do his duty by me.' And he shall say, 'I will not take her.' And they used to say this in the Holy Language: 'His brother's widow shall go up to him in the presence of the elders; she shall pull his sandal off his foot and spit in his face' – such spittle as can be seen by the judges; 'and she shall declare: "Thus we requite the man who will not build up his brother's family." ' Thus far they used to quote (the prescribed words). But when R. Hyrcanus under the terebinth in Kefar Etam rehearsed it and completed it to the end of the section, the rule was established to complete the section. (To say the words) 'His family shall be known in Israel as the House of the Unsandalled Man' was a duty that fell upon the judges and not upon the disciples. But R. Judah says: 'It was a duty that fell upon all those who stood there to cry out, "The man that has his shoe loosed! The man that has his shoe loosed! The man that has his shoe loosed!" '

Cf. 7.3.

2.20 Ket. xiii.1

There were two judges of *gezeroth* ['decisions' or 'ordinances'; but n.b. var. 'robberies'] in Jerusalem, Admon and Ḥanan b. Abishalom. Ḥanan gave two decisions, Admon gave seven. If a man goes overseas and a wife claims maintenance, Ḥanan says, 'Let her make the claim [lit. 'swear'] at the end, and not at the beginning.' The sons of the high priests (*bne khnim gdwlim*) disputed this, and said: 'Let her swear both at the beginning and at the end.' R. Dosa b. Harkinas said: 'It is as they say.' Rn. Joḥanan b. Zakkai said: 'Ḥanan spoke correctly. She shall only make the claim at the end.'

2.21 Sot. iii.4

R. Joshua says: 'A woman desires one *qab* and enjoyment more than nine *qabim* and *perishut*.' He used to say: 'A foolish saint (*ḥasid*), a wicked man with cunning, a woman who is *prushah*, and the wounds (*makkot*) of those who are *prushim*, these wear out the world.'

Cf. 4.22; 5.14.

2.22 Sot. ix.10–15

[10] Joḥanan the High Priest did away with the avowal concerning the tithe. He made an end also of the 'Awakeners' and the 'Stunners'. Until his days the hammer used to smite Jerusalem; and in his days none needed to enquire concerning *demai*-produce.

[11] When the Sanhedrin ceased, singing ceased at the wedding feasts, as it is written, 'No one shall drink wine to the sound of song' [Is. xxiv.9].

[12] When the First Prophets died, Urim and Thummim ceased. When the Temple was destroyed the Shamir-worm ceased and the honey of Zofim; and faithful men (*anshe amnah*) came to an end, as it is written, 'Help, Lord, for loyalty is no more' [Ps. xii.1]. Rabban Simeon b. Gamaliel says in the name of R. Joshua: 'Since the day that the Temple was destroyed there has been no day without its curse; and the dew has not fallen in blessing and the fruits have lost their savour.' R. Jose says: 'The fruits have also lost their fatness.'

[13] R. Simeon b. Eleazar says: '(When) purity (ceased in Israel it) took away the flavour and the fragrance; (when) the Tithes (ceased they) took away the fatness of the corn; and the Ḥakamim say [but some MSS om. Ḥakamim] fornication and sorceries have made an end of them all.'

[14] During the war of Vespasian they forbade the crowns of the bridegrooms and the (wedding) drum. During the war of Titus they forbade the crowns of the brides and that a man should teach his son Greek. In the last war they forbade the bride to go forth in a litter inside the city; but our Rabbis permitted the bride to go forth in a litter inside the city.

[15] When R. Meir died there were no more makers of parables. When Ben Azzai died there were no more diligent students. When Ben Zoma died there were no more expounders (*hadrshnim*). When R. Joshua died goodness departed from the world. When Rabban Simeon b. Gamaliel died the locust came and troubles grew many. When R. Eleazar b. Azariah died wealth departed from the Ḥakamim. When R. Akiba died the glory of the Law ceased. When R. Ḥanina b. Dosa died the men of good deeds (*anshe ma'aseh*) ceased. When R. Jose Katnutha died there were no more saintly ones (*ḥasidim*). And why was his name called Katnutha? Because he was the least of the saintly ones (*ḥasidim*). When Rabban Joḥanan b. Zakkai died the splendour of wisdom ceased. When Rabban Gamaliel the Elder died, the glory of the Law ceased and purity and abstinence died (*thrah uphrishut*). When R. Ishmael b. Piabi died the splendour of the priesthood ceased. When Rabbi died, humility and the shunning of sin ceased.

R. Phineḥas b. Jair says: 'When the Temple was destroyed the *ḥaberim* and the freemen were put to shame and walked with lowered head, and the men of good works (*anshe ma'aseh*) waxed feeble; and men of violence and men of loud tongue prevailed.' And (now) there is none that expounds (to Israel) and none that seeks, and none that enquires. On whom can we stay ourselves? On our Father in heaven. R. Eliezer the Great says: 'Since the day that the Temple was destroyed the Ḥakamim [lit. *ḥkimai*] began to be like school-teachers, and the school-teachers like synagogue-servants, and the synagogue-servants like the people of the land; and the people of the land waxed feeble, and there was none to seek.' On whom can we stay ourselves? On our Father in heaven. With the footprints of the Messiah presumption shall increase and dearth reach its height; the vine shall yield its fruit but the wine shall be costly; and the heathen shall fall into heresy and there shall be none to utter reproof. The council-chamber shall be given to fornication. Galilee shall be laid to waste and Gablan shall be made desolate; and the people of the frontier shall go about from city to city with none to show pity on them. The wisdom of the Scribes (*ḥkmth sopherim*) shall become empty and they that shun sin shall be deemed contemptible, and truth shall nowhere be found. Children shall shame the elders, and the elders shall rise up before the children, 'for son maligns father, daughter rebels against mother, daughter-in-law against mother-in-law, and a man's enemies are of his own household' [Mic. vii.6]. The face of this generation is as the face of a dog, and the son will not be put to shame by his father. On whom can we stay ourselves? On our Father in heaven. R. Phineḥas b. Jair says: 'Heedfulness leads to cleanliness, and cleanliness leads to purity, and purity leads to abstinence (*prishut*), and abstinence leads to holiness, and holiness leads to humility, and humility leads to the shunning of sin, and the shunning of sin leads to saintliness (*ḥsidut*), and saintliness leads to the holy spirit, and the holy spirit leads to the resurrection of the dead. And the resurrection of the dead shall come through Elijah of blessed memory.' Amen.

For Joḥanan (§10*), cf.* 1.2 *and the further references. For the last paragraph, see* 4.31.

2.23 San. vii.2

The ordinance of those who are to be burnt (is this): they set him in dung up to his arm-pits and put a towel of coarse stuff within one of soft stuff and wrapped it around his neck; one (witness) pulled one end towards him and the other pulled one end towards him until he opened his mouth; a wick was kindled and thrown into his mouth, and it went down to his stomach and burnt his entrails. R. Judah says: 'If thus he died at their hands they would not have fulfilled the ordinance of burning; but, rather, they must open his mouth with tongs by force and kindle the wick and throw it into his mouth, and it goes down to his stomach and burns his entrails.' R. Eliezer b. Zadok said: 'It happened once that a priest's daughter committed adultery [cf. Lev. xxi.9] and they encompassed her with bundles of branches and burnt her.' They said to him: 'Because the court at that time had not right knowledge.'

Cf. 3.15; 4.30.

2.24 San. xi.3

Greater strictness applies to the words of the scribes (*dibre sopherim*) than to the words of Torah. If a man says, 'There is no obligation to wear *tephillin* (phylacteries)', so that he transgresses words of Torah, he is free; (if he says), 'There are five partitions (not four)', so that he adds to the words of the scribes, he is guilty.

On the strictness attaching to the words of the scribes, cf. 2.30; 2.36; 4.16; 5.1. *For general references, see the Index under Scribes and dibre sopherim.*

2.25 Makk. i.6

False witnesses are put to death only after judgement has been given. For the Sadducees used to say: 'Not unless he (the one falsely accused) has been put to death, as it is written, "Life for life" [Dt. xix.21].' The Ḥakamim answered: 'Is it not also written, "You shall treat him as he intended to treat his fellow" [Dt. xix.19]? Thus his brother must still be alive.' If so, why was it written, 'Life for life'? Could it be that they were put to death so soon as their evidence was received (and proved false)? But Scripture says, 'Life for life'; thus they are not put to death until judgement (of death) has been given (against the falsely accused).

Cf. 3.14; 4.18; 4.33; 6.10; *and cf. also* 1.2 *(*294*).*

2.26 Aboth i.1–4

[1] Moses received Torah from Sinai, and committed it to Joshua, and Joshua to the elders, and the elders to the prophets, and the prophets committed it to the men of the Great Synagogue. They said three things: be deliberate in judgement (*din*), establish many disciples, and make a fence (*syag*) for Torah.

[2] Simeon the Just was of the remnants of the Great Synagogue. He used to say: 'On three things the world is sustained: on Torah, on (Temple-) service, and on deeds of active piety.'

[3] Antigonus of Socho received (Torah) from Simeon the Just.

He used to say: 'Be not like servants who minister to the master for the sake of receiving reward, but be like servants that minister to the master without a view to receiving reward. And let the fear of heaven be upon you.'

[4] Jose b. Joezer of Zeredah and Jose b. Joḥanan, a man of Jerusalem, received (Torah) from them. Jose b. Joezer used to say: 'Let your house be a house of meeting for the Ḥakamim, and sit in the dust of their feet and drink thirstily their words.'

On §1, *cf.* 3.18, *and see also* 2.27. *On* §2, *cf.* 6.17. *On* §3 *see* 6.1; 6.2; *note also the variant in the Geniza Fragment, 'with a view to not receiving a reward' (A. I. Katsh, 'Unpublished Geniza Fragments of Pirke Aboth in the Antonin Geniza Collection in Leningrad'*, J.Q.R. LXI, 1970, 1–14).

2.27 Aboth iii.13

R. Aqiba said: '. . . Tradition (*mswrth*) is a fence for Torah, tithes are a fence for riches, vows are a fence for *prishut*, a fence for wisdom is silence.'

2.28 Men. vi.2

The meal-offering of the priests, and the meal-offering of the anointed priest, and the meal-offering offered with the drink-offerings fall (wholly) to the altar, and the priests have no share in them; here the right of the altar exceeds the right of the priests. The Two Loaves and the Shewbread belong to the priests and the altar has no share in them; here the right of the priests exceeds the right of the altar.

Cf. 7.7.

2.29 Men. x.3

How was it (the *'omer*) made ready? The messengers of the Bet Din used to go out on the eve of the festival day and tie the corn in bunches while it was yet unreaped to make it the easier to reap; and the towns nearby all assembled there together that it might be reaped with much ceremony (*b'sq gdwl*). When it grew dark he called out, 'Is the sun set?', and they answered, 'Yes.' 'Is the sun set?', and they answered, 'Yes.' 'With this sickle?', and they answered, 'Yes.' 'With this sickle?', and they answered, 'Yes.' 'In this basket?', and they answered 'Yes.' 'In this basket?', and they answered 'Yes.' At the close of a Sabbath he called out, 'On this Sabbath?', and they answered, 'Yes.' 'On this Sabbath?', and they answered, 'Yes.' 'Shall I reap?', and they answered, 'Reap.' 'Shall I reap?', and they answered, 'Reap.' He used to call out three times for every matter, and they answered, 'Yes', 'Yes', 'Yes.' Why was all this? Because of the Boethusians who used to say: 'The *'Omer* may not be reaped at the close of a festival day.'

Cf. also 2.17 (4) *and the further references for the associated controversy over the date of Shabuot.*

2.30 Kel. xiii.7

If hooked iron levers of Ashkelon were broken but the hooks remained, they are susceptible to uncleanness. If a pitch-fork, winnowing-fan, or rake, or even a comb, has lost one of its teeth and another of metal has been made for it, they become susceptible to uncleanness. Concerning all this, R. Joshua said: 'A new thing the scribes have innovated, and I have nothing with which to answer.'

On the 'word of the scribes' see 2.24 *and the further references.*

2.31 Par. iii.3

When they (the children) came to the Temple Mount (in preparation for the burning of the Red Heifer) they alighted. Beneath both the Temple Mount and the courts of the Temple was a hollowed space for fear of any grave down in the depths. At the entrance of the Temple Court was set ready a jar of the (ashes of) the sin-offering. They brought a male from among the sheep, tied a rope between its horns, and tied at the end (of the rope) a stick with a cone, and threw it (the cone) into the jar. The sheep was struck so that it jumped backwards (and spilled the ashes), and a child took (some of the ashes) and scattered enough to be visible on the water. R. Jose says: 'Give not the Sadducees occasion to rebel, but, rather, one (of the children) took (the ashes directly) from the jar and made ready with them.'

Cf. 2.32; 3.16; 4.11; 4.19; 4.34; 5.8.

2.32 Par. iii.6–8

[6] They made a causeway from the Temple Mount to the Mount of Olives, an arched way built over an arched way, with an arch directly above each pier (of the arch below), for fear of any grave in the depths below. By it the priest who was to burn the Heifer, and the Heifer, and all who aided him went forth to the Mount of Olives.

[7] If the Heifer refused to go forth they may not send out with her a black heifer lest any say, 'They slaughtered a black heifer'; nor another red heifer, lest any say, 'They slaughtered two.' R. Jose says: 'It was not for this reason, but because it is written, "And she shall be taken outside" [Num. xix.3], by herself.' And the elders of Israel used to go forth before them on foot to the Mount of Olives. There was a place of immersion there; and they had (first) rendered unclean the priest who should burn the Heifer, because of the Sadducees: that they should not be able to say, 'It must be performed only by them on whom the sun has set.'

[8] They laid their hands upon him and said, 'My lord the High Priest, immerse yourself this once.' He went down and immersed himself and came up and dried himself . . .

See 2.31 *and the further references.*

2.33 Toh. iv.12

A condition of doubt about animals ordinarily killed (*ḥullin*) concerns the cleanness (*tohorot*) of *prishut* . . .

2.34 Nidd. iv.2

The daughters of the Sadducees, if they follow after the ways of their fathers, are deemed to be like the women of the Samaritans (*kutim*); but if they have separated themselves (*parashu*) and follow after the ways of the Israelites, they are deemed to be like the women of the Israelites. R. Jose says: 'They are always deemed to be like the women of the Israelites unless they separate themselves and follow after the ways of their fathers.'

Cf. 3.17 *(1f.)*.

2.35 Nidd. x.6

At first they used to say: 'She who continues in "the blood which requires purification" [Lev. xii.4] was permitted to pour out the water for the Passover offering.' But they changed and said: 'For the hallowed things (*lqdshim*) she is like one who has been in contact with one who suffered uncleanness from contact with the dead.' This is according to Bet Hillel. Bet Shammai said: 'Even like one who has suffered uncleanness from contact with the dead.'

2.36 Yad. iii.2

Whatsoever renders Heave-offering invalid can convey second-grade uncleanness to the hands; the one hand can render the other unclean. So R. Joshua. But the Ḥakamim say: 'That which suffers second-grade uncleanness cannot convey second-grade uncleanness to anything else.' He said to them, 'But do not the Holy Scriptures, which suffer second-grade uncleanness, render the hands unclean?' They answered, 'You may infer nothing about the words of the Law from the words of the scribes (*dibre sopherim*) and nothing about the words of the scribes from the words of the Law, and nothing about the words of the scribes from (other) words of the scribes.'

On the 'words of the scribes', see 2.24 *and the further references.*

2.37 Yad. iii.5

If the writing in a scroll was erased yet there still remained eighty-five letters, as many as are in the paragraph 'Whenever the ark began to move' [Num. x.35f.], it still renders the hands unclean. A (single) written sheet (in a scroll of the Scriptures) in which are written eighty-five letters, as many as are in the paragraph 'Whenever the ark began to move' renders the hands unclean. All the Holy Scriptures render the hands unclean. The Song of Songs and Ecclesiastes render the hands unclean. R. Judah says: 'The Song of Songs renders the hands unclean, but about Ecclesiastes there is dissension.' R. Jose says: 'Ecclesiastes does not render the hands unclean, and about the Song of Songs there is dissension.' R. Simeon says: 'Ecclesiastes is one of the things about which the Bet Shammai adopted the more lenient, and the Bet Hillel the more stringent ruling.' R. Simeon b. Azzai said: 'I have heard a tradition from the seventy-two elders on the day when they made R. Eleazar b. Azariah head of the scholars' assembly (*yshibah*), that the Song of Songs and Ecclesiastes both render the hands unclean.' R. Aqiba said: 'God forbid! no man in Israel ever disputed about the Song of Songs (that he should say) that it does not render the hands unclean, for all the ages are not worth the day on which the Song of Songs was given to Israel; for all the Writings are holy, but the Song of Songs is the Holy of Holies. And if anything was in dispute the dispute was about Ecclesiastes alone.' R. Joḥanan b. Joshua, the son of R. Aqiba's father-in-law, said: 'According to the words of Ben Azzai so did they dispute and so did they decide.'

2.38 Yad. iv.6–8

The Sadducees say, 'We cry out against you, *prushim*, for you say, "The Holy Scriptures render the hands unclean", (and) "The writings of Hamiram do not render the hands unclean." ' Rabban Joḥanan b. Zakkai said, 'Have we nothing against the *prushim* except this? For they say, "The bones of an ass are clean, and the bones of Joḥanan the High Priest are unclean." ' They said to him, 'As is our love for them so is their uncleanness – that no man make spoons of the bones of his father or mother.' He said to them, 'Even so the Holy Scriptures: as is our love for them so is their uncleanness;

(whereas) the writings of Hamiram which are held in no account do not render the hands unclean.'

The Sadducees say, 'We cry out against you, *prushim*, for you declare clean an unbroken stream of liquid (*nizzoq*).' The *prushim* say, 'We cry out against you, Sadducees, for you declare clean a channel of water that flows from a burial ground.' The Sadducees say, 'We cry out against you, *prushim*, for you say, "If my ox or my ass have done an injury they are culpable, but if my bondman or my bondwoman have done an injury they are not culpable": if, in the case of my ox or my ass (about which no commandments are laid upon me) I am responsible for the injury that they do, how much more in the case of my bondman or my bondwoman (about whom certain commandments are laid upon me) must I be responsible for the injury that they do?' They said to them, 'No. As you argue concerning my ox or my ass (which have no understanding) would you likewise argue concerning my bondman or my bondwoman which have understanding? If I provoke him to anger he may go and set fire to another's stack of corn, and it is I that must make restitution.'

A Galilean heretic said, 'I cry out against you, *prushim*, for you write in a bill of divorce the name of the ruler together with the name of Moses.' The *prushim* said, 'We cry out against you, Galilean heretic, for you write the name of the ruler together with the Name (of God) on the (same) page, and, moreover, you write the name of the ruler above, and the Name (of God) below; as it is written, "And Pharaoh said, Who is the Lord that I should obey him and let Israel go?" [Exod. v.2]. But when he was smitten what did he say? "The Lord is in the right" [Exod. ix.27].'

On the cleanness of a scripture scroll (§6*), cf.* 2.36; 2.37. *For* §8, *cf.* 7.6. *In* §8, *'Galilean' is probably correct, but some texts have 'Sadducee'.*

TOSEFTA

3.1 Ber. iii.25

The eighteen blessings (*shemoneh ʿesreh berakoth*), which the Ḥakamim refer to, correspond to the eighteen mentions of the Divine Name (*azkrot*) which are in the psalm (beginning): 'Ascribe to the Lord, O sons of might . . . ' [Ps. xxix.1]. What pertains to the *minim* he (the one reciting) includes in what pertains to [i.e., in the blessing pertaining to] the *prushim*, and what pertains to the *gerim* he includes in what pertains to (the blessing pertaining to) the *zeqenim*, and what pertains to David he includes in 'the builder of Jerusalem.' If anyone says these on their own (without making the inclusions), he has still fulfilled his obligation.

Cf. 5.2. *Note the comment of S. Liebermann (*Tosefta Kifshuta, *p.* 54*), on this passage, who argued that* prushim *are those who desert the community in time of trouble, and gave further examples of passages in which this meaning can be discerned.*

3.2 Dem. ii.2f., 10–14

He who takes on himself four things, they receive as a *ḥaber*: not to give *terumah* or tithes to the *ʿam haAreẓ*, and not to make ready his ritually prepared food with (in the presence of) the *ʿam haAreẓ*, and to eat ordinary food (*ḥullin*) in purity; he who takes on himself to be trustworthy (*neʾeman*), tithes what he eats and what he sells and what he buys, and does not stay as a guest with an *ʿam haAreẓ*; so according to R. Meir. The Ḥakamim say: 'If he stays as a guest with the *ʿam haAreẓ* he can still be trustworthy (*neʾeman*).' R. Meir said to them: 'If he is not trustworthy in respect to himself, how can he be considered so in respect to others? . . . '

[3] The *ʿam haAreẓ* who takes on himself the obligation (*dbr*) of a *ḥaber* and is suspect in one single matter is suspect in all; so according to R. Meir. The Ḥakamim say: 'He is only suspect in the one matter alone.'

[10] He who comes to take (the obligation) on himself, if he used to practise privately from the beginning, they receive him, and after

that they instruct him (*mlmdin*); and if not, they instruct him, and after that receive him . . .

[11] They accept him (as a *ḥaber*) if he undertakes to observe *kenaphayim* and after that accept him for [i.e., 'as one who will observe'] *tohorot*. If a man said, 'I accept on myself (the obligations) for *kenaphayim* alone', they receive him. If he accepts on himself (the obligations) for *tohorot* and does not accept (the obligations) for *kenaphayim* in addition to *tohorot*, he is not trustworthy (*ne'eman*) even for *tohorot*.

[12] How long (must he practise levitical purity) before they receive him? Bet Shammai say: 'For liquids thirty days, for clothing twelve months.' Bet Hillel say: 'In both cases, thirty days.'

[13] He who comes to accept (the obligations) on himself, even if he is fully trained (*talmid ḥakam*), it is necessary for him to accept the obligations on himself; but (in the case of) the *ḥakam* who sits in the assembly (*yshibah*), it is not necessary for him to accept (the obligations) on himself, since he undertook them when he was made a member. Abba Saul said: 'In the case of the *talmid ḥakam* also, there is no need for him to accept (the obligations) on himself, nor even for those who enter membership [lit. 'who accept in his presence'] before him . . . '

[14] He who undertakes (the obligations) before the *ḥaburah*, there is no need for his sons and servants to undertake them before the *ḥaburah*, but can undertake them before him . . .

Cf. 2.2 *and the further references.*

3.3 Shab. i.15

Bet Shammai say: 'A man who suffers from emission who is *parush* (*zab parush*) should not eat with a *zab* who is *'am haAreẓ*.' But Bet Hillel allow it.

Cf. 4.3.

3.4 Yoma i.8

Why did he turn aside (√*prsh*) and weep? Because he had to be put on oath. Why did they turn aside (√*prsh*) and weep? Because they had to put him on oath. And why did they need to put him on oath? It was because of a certain Boethusian (high priest) who prepared the incense on the outside, and the cloud of incense went forth and shook the whole temple. (He did so because) the Boethusians used to say, 'He should prepare the incense on the outside, as it is said: " . . . and the cloud of incense will hide . . . " [Lev. xvi.13b].' The Ḥakamim said to them: 'Is it not already said: "He shall put the incense on the fire before the Lord" [Lev. xvi.13]? Everyone who prepares the incense must always do so within (the Holy of Holies).' But in that case, why is it said, ' . . . and the cloud of incense will hide . . . ' [but n.b. variant text]? It teaches that he puts on it a smoke-raiser [i.e., grass or a plant which makes smoke], and if he did not put a smoke-raiser on it, he is liable to death. When he (the Boethusian) went forth [or 'came out'], he said to his father: 'All the days of your lives you (and your fellows) used to interpret it but never enacted it until I stood up and performed it (according to our interpretation).' His father replied: 'Although we interpret it, we do not enact it, but we listen to the words of the Ḥakamim (*dbre ḥkmim*). It will amaze me if you live.' Not three days had gone by before they put him in his grave.

Cf. 2.11 *and the further references.*

3.5 Sukk. iii.1

The *lulab* (palm-branch) takes precedence over the Sabbath at the beginning (of the festival), and the willows (similarly) at the end. It happened once that the Boethusians covered the willows with large rocks on the eve of the Sabbath. The *'amme haAreẓ* discovered them and pulled them out and took them from under the rocks on the Sabbath, because the Boethusians do not accept that the beating with the willows takes precedence over the Sabbath. (The precedence of) the willows is a *halakah* which goes back to Moses from Sinai, but Abba Saul said: 'It is from Torah, as it says, "And willows [emphasising plural] from the riverside" [Lev. xxiii.40], one (for *lulab*, one) for the altar.'

Cf. 4.14; 5.6; 5.8; *and see also* 1.3.

3.6 Sukk. iii.16

It happened on one occasion that a certain (*aḥd*) Boethusian poured out the libation over his feet, and all the people pelted him with their *ethrogim*; and the horn of the altar was damaged, and worship stopped that day until a lump of salt was brought which they put on it lest the altar should appear damaged . . .

Cf. 1.3 *and the further references.*

3.7 R.H. i.15

At first they accepted the witness of the new moon from any man. Once, the Boethusians hired two witnesses to come and mislead the Ḥakamim, because the Boethusians do not accept that the feast of Weeks (*'ẓrth*) can fall except after the Sabbath. One witness came and gave his testimony and went away. The second came and said: 'I was going up the ascent of Adumim and I saw it crouched between two rocks, its head like that of a calf, its ears like those of a hind. I saw it and I was frightened and I fell backwards, and here are two hundred *zuzim* wrapped in my cloak [some MSS 'purse'] . . .'

Cf. 2.14 *and the further references.*

3.8 Ḥag. iii.8

There was only conflict over *semikah* (laying on of hands). There were five *zugoth* (pairs): three of the first *zugoth* who said there should be no *semikah* were *nasi* [lit. pl. *nesi'im*, president], and their seconds [i.e., deputies] (who opposed them) were *ab* [lit. *aboth*] *bet din*; two of the later *zugoth* who said there should be no *semikah* were *nasi* and their seconds (who opposed them) were *ab bet din.*

Cf. 2.16.

3.9 Ḥag. iii.35

On one occasion they purified the *menorah* on *yom tob*, and the Sadducees said: 'Come and see the *prushim* purifying the orb of the moon.'

Cf. 5.12.

3.10 Sot. xiii.10

'The Stunners' are those who incise the calf between the horns as they do in idolatry. Joḥanan the high priest [n.b.var. 'Joḥanan b. Zakkai'] said to them: 'How long will you feed the altar with *terefoth*?'

For Joḥanan, cf. 1.2 *and the further references.*

3.11 Sot. xv.11,12

After the destruction of the Temple, *prushim* increased in Israel, and they would not eat flesh or drink wine. R. Joshua joined in discussion with them, and said: 'My sons, for what reason do you not eat flesh?' They replied: 'Shall we eat flesh from what used to be offered daily (as Tamid) on the altar, but has now ceased?' He said: 'For what reason do you not drink wine?' They answered: 'Shall we drink wine from what used to be poured out as libations on the altar, but now has ceased?'

[12] He replied: 'Also figs and fruits we should not eat, since first-fruits (*bikkurim*) are taken from them on the feast of Weeks . . .' He said to them: 'Not to mourn at all is not possible, because the blow has fallen, and yet to mourn excessively is not possible.' The Ḥakamim therefore have ordained thus: 'A man may stucco his house, but he should leave a little bare as a memorial of Jerusalem.'

Cf. 4.26.

3.12 San. iii.4

Abba Saul said: 'There are two valleys ['open places'?] in Jerusalem, the lower and the upper. The lower was consecrated by all the (necessary) methods, but the upper was not consecrated until the exiles returned, when there was no king and no Urim and no Thummim. In the lower valley, which was consecrated completely, the *'amme haAreẓ* used to eat the lesser holy things, as did the *ḥaberim* also, except for the second tithe. In the upper valley, which was not consecrated completely, the *'amme haAreẓ* used to eat the lesser holy things, except for the second tithe, but the *ḥaberim* ate neither. Why was the upper valley not consecrated? Because it was a vulnerable part of Jerusalem which could easily be over-run.'

For relations between ḥaberim *and* 'amme haAreẓ, *see* 2.2 *and the further references.*

3.13 San. iv.7

R. Jose said: 'Ezra would have been approved as the one through whom Torah would have been given had not Moses preceded him: about Moses, a "going up" is mentioned, and about Ezra, the same, as it says, "And Moses went up to God" [Ex. xix.3], and of Ezra, "And he, Ezra, went up from Babylon" [Ezra vii.6]. As the "going up" of Moses taught Torah to Israel, as it is written, "The Lord commanded me 'At that time the Lord charged me to teach you statutes and laws' " [Dt. iv.14], so the "going up" of Ezra taught Torah to Israel, as it is written, "For Ezra had devoted himself to the study and observance of the law of the Lord, and to do it, and to teaching statute and ordinance in Israel" [Ezra vii.10].'

On the importance of Ezra, cf. 5.9; 9.4.

3.14 San. vi.6

Witnesses can never be confirmed as false until the trial has been completed. They cannot be scourged, fined, or executed, until the trial has been completed. One of the witnesses cannot be confirmed as false without the other, nor can one be scourged, or executed, or fined, without the other. R. Judah ben Tabbai said: 'May I never see the Consolation if I did not execute one false witness in order to root out from the hearts of the Boethusians the view which they used to express, that a false witness is not to be executed until the accused has been executed.' Simeon ben Shetaḥ said to him: 'May I never see the consolation if you have not shed innocent blood; for Torah says: "Sentence of death shall be carried out on the testimony of two or of three witnesses" [Dt. xvii.6]. Just as there are two witnesses, so also there must be two false witnesses.' At that moment Judah ben Tabbai took it on himself not to teach *halakah* except in agreement with Simeon ben Shetaḥ.

Cf. 2.25 *and the further references.*

3.15 San. ix.11

R. Eliezer b. R. Zadok said: 'When I was a child I was once riding on my father's shoulder, and I saw a priest's daughter who had committed adultery, and they surrounded her with bundles of branches [or 'vine-branches'] and burned her.' They said to him: 'You were a child, and a child cannot give evidence.'

Cf. 2.23 *and the further references.*

3.16 Par. iii.8

It once happened that a certain Sadducee came, after the sun had set on him, to burn the Red Heifer, and Rn. Joḥanan ben Zakkai knew about it, and came and put his two hands on him and said: 'High priest, how worthy you are to be high priest: go and immerse yourself again.' And he went and immersed himself, and returned. When he returned, he cut his ear; he said to him: 'Ben Zakkai, when I have time for you –.' '*If* you have time', he retorted. Not three days went by before they were putting him in his grave. His father came to Rn. Joḥanan ben Zakkai and said to him: 'My son has time' [or, 'and said, My son has no leisure (to take revenge)'].

Cf. 2.31 *and the further references.*

3.17 Nidd. v.1–3

The daughters of the Samaritans are (deemed unclean as) menstruants from their cradle; and the Samaritans convey uncleanness to what lies beneath them in like degree as (he that has a flux conveys uncleanness) to what lies above him, since they have connection with menstruants . . .

[2] The daughters of the Sadducees, as long as they walk in the ways of their fathers are like Samaritan women (*kutim*). If they separate (*prshu*) to the ways of Israel they are like Israel.

[3] There was once a certain Sadducee woman who conversed with a high priest when some spittle fell from her mouth and dropped on the clothes of the high priest. The face of the high priest turned yellow, and they came and asked her and she said: 'High priest, although we are wives of Sadducees, everything is taken to a *ḥakam* for decision.' R. Jose said: 'We know the Sadducee women better than anyone else, because they all ask a *ḥakam* for a decision, except for one of them, and she died.'

For §§1 *and* 2, *cf.* 2.34; *for* §3, *cf.* 4.37.

3.18 Yad. ii.16

R. Eliezer said: '. . . I received from Rn. Joḥanan b. Zakkai, who received it from the *zugoth* (pairs), and the *zugoth* from the prophets, and the prophets from Moses, a *halakah* going back to Moses from Sinai, that the tithes for the poor can be apportioned from Ammon and Moab in the seventh year.'

On the chain of tradition, cf. 2.26.

3.19 Yad. ii.20

The Boethusians say: 'We cry out against you, *prushim*, for maintaining that the daughter of my son, who is directly descended from my son who is directly descended from myself, inherits from me; how much more should my daughter, who is directly descended from myself, inherit from me.' The *prushim* say: 'Not so: if you agree (as you do) in the case of the daughter of the son who divides the estate with the brothers (of the deceased man), you should agree (with us) in the case of the daughter who does not divide with her brothers.' The ones who immerse themselves early (*toble saḥar*) said: 'We cry out against you, *prushim*, because you mention the name of God from the body which has uncleanness in it.'

Cf. 4.27; 5.16; 7.4.

BABYLONIAN TALMUD

4.1 Ber. 14b, 15a

R. Joḥanan said: 'If one desires to accept upon himself the yoke of the kingdom of heaven in the most complete manner, [15a] he should relieve himself and wash his hands and put on *tephillin* and recite the *Shema'* and say the *tephillah*: this is the complete acknowledgement of the kingdom of heaven.' R. Ḥiyya b. Abba said in the name of R. Joḥanan: 'If a man relieves himself and washes his hands and puts on *tephillin* and recites the *Shema'* and says the *tephillah*, Scripture accounts it to him as if he had built an altar and offered a sacrifice upon it, as it is written, "I will wash my hands in innocence to join in procession round your altar, O Lord" [Ps. xxvi.6].' Raba said to him: 'Does not your honour think that it is as if he had bathed himself, since it is written, "I will wash in purity", and it is not written, "I will wash my hands"?' Rabina said to Raba: 'Sir, pray look at this student who has come from the West (Palestine) and who says: "If one has no water for washing his hands, he can rub his hands with earth or with a pebble or with sawdust".' He replied: 'He is quite correct. Is it written, I will wash in water? It is written: In cleanliness – with anything which cleans.' For R. Ḥisda cursed anyone who went looking for water at the time of prayer. This applies to the recital of the *Shema'*, but for the *tephillah* one may go looking. How far? As far as a *parasang*. This is the case in front of him, but in the rear, he may not go back even a *mil*. (From which is to be deduced), a *mil* he may not go back; but less that a *mil* he may go back.

Cf. 2.17 *(*5*) and the further references. On the 'yoke of the kingdom', see* 6.17.

4.2 Ber. 22a

When Ze'iri came (from Palestine), he said: 'They have abolished the ritual ablution.' Some report him to have said: 'They have abolished the washing of hands.' The one who reports, 'They have abolished the ritual ablution', concurs with R. Judah b. Bathyra.

The one who reports, 'They have abolished the washing of hands', is in accord with R. Ḥisda, who cursed anyone who went looking for water at the hour of prayer. Our Rabbis taught: 'A man who has had recent emission (*bʿl qri*) on whom nine *qabs* of water have been thrown is clean . . .' R. Joshua b. Levi said: 'What is the sense of the morning bathers (*toble saḥrain*)?' What sense? It was he himself who said that a *baʿal qeri* is forbidden (to occupy himself) with the words of the Torah! What he meant is this: What is the sense of bathing in forty *se'ahs* when one can make shift with nine *qabs*? What is the sense of going right in when throwing the water over one is sufficient? R. Ḥanina said: 'They put up a very valuable fence (*gdr*) by this, as it has been taught: Once a man enticed a woman to commit an offence and she said to him: "Vagabond, have you forty *se'ahs* to bathe in?" He at once desisted.' R. Huna said to the disciples: 'My masters, why do you make so light of this bathing? Is it because of the cold? You can use the baths!' R. Ḥisda said to him: 'Can ablution be performed in hot baths?' He replied: 'R. Adda b. Ahabah is of the same opinion as you.' R. Zeʿira used to sit in a tub of water in the baths and say to his servant, 'Go and fetch nine *qabs* and throw it over me.' R. Ḥiyya b. Abba said to him: 'Why, sir, do you take this trouble, seeing that you are sitting in (that quantity of) water?' He replied: 'The nine *qabs* must be like the forty *se'ahs*: just as the forty *se'ahs* are for immersion and not for throwing, so the nine *qabs* are for throwing and not for immersion.'

Cf. 2.17 *(*5*) and the further references.*

4.3 Shab. 13a

A *zab* who is *parush* may not eat with a *zab* who is *ʿam haAreẓ*, lest he cause him to become familiar with him. But what does it matter if he does cause him to become familiar with him? Rather say: lest he offer him unclean food to eat. But does not a *zab* who is *parush* (by definition) eat unclean food? Abaye said: 'For fear lest he provide him with unfit (untithed) food.' Raba said: 'The majority of the *ʿamme haAreẓ* do render tithes, but lest he becomes familiar with him and provides him with unclean food when he is once again clean.'

Cf. 2.2; 3.3.

4.4 Shab. 14b

'And the hands': did the pupils (*tlmidey*) of Shammai and Hillel decree this? Shammai and Hillel themselves decreed it; for it was taught: Jose b. Joezer, a man of Zeredah, and Jose b. Joḥanan, a man of Jerusalem, decreed uncleanness in respect of the land of the heathens, and in respect of vessels of glass. Simeon b. Shetaḥ instituted *ketubah* [i.e., the use of the marriage settlement by the husband in his affairs] for women, and decreed uncleanness with respect to vessels of metal. Shammai and Hillel decreed uncleanness with respect to the hands. And if you say, Shammai and his company (*si'tho*), and Hillel and his company, in fact Rab Jehudah said in Samuel's name: 'They decreed eighteen things, and they differed in eighteen things, whereas Hillel and Shammai differed only in three places [i.e., they only needed to decree where they differed]...' Yet surely Solomon decreed it? For R. Jehudah said in Samuel's name, 'When Solomon instituted *'erubin* and the washing of hands, a *bath qol* came forth and said: "My son, if you are wise at heart my heart in its turn will be glad" [Prov. xxiii.15]; "Be wise, my son, then you will bring joy to my heart, and I shall be able to forestall my critics" [Prov. xxvii.11].' Solomon came and decreed for holy things [i.e., washing of hands before sacrifice], and they came and decreed for *terumah*.

On the enactments of Simeon b. Shetaḥ, see also 4.5; 5.15. *On* 'erubin, *see* 2.6. *On washing of hands, see* 2.17 *and further references.*

4.5 Shab. 16b

'Simeon b. Shetaḥ instituted *ketubah* for women, and he decreed uncleanness for vessels of metal': but vessels of metal are Biblical, for it is written, 'whether gold, or silver, etc.' [Num. xxxi.23]. It was only necessary in respect of former uncleanness, for Rab Jehudah said in Rab's name: 'It happened once that Queen Shal-Ẓion made a banquet for her son and all her vessels were defiled. Thereupon she broke them and gave them to the goldsmith, who melted them down and manufactured new utensils of them. But the Ḥakamim said: "They revert to their former uncleanness."' What is the reason? They were concerned there to provide a fence (*gdr*) against the water of separation [i.e., to provide against its being abandoned by the expedient of melting down and remaking].

Cf. 1.4 *(and the further references) for Salome. On the enactments of Simeon b. Shetaḥ, see* 4.4.

4.6 Shab. 31a

Our Rabbis taught: It happened once that a certain non-Jew (*nkri*) came to Shammai and said: 'How many Toroth have you?' He said, 'Two: written Torah and Torah transmitted by mouth (*torah shebe'al peh*).' 'I believe you with respect to the Written, but not with respect to the Oral Torah: make me a proselyte on condition that you teach me the Written Torah (only).' (But) he scolded and repulsed him in anger. When he went before Hillel, he accepted him as a proselyte. On the first day he taught him, Alef, beth, gimmel, daleth; the following day he reversed (them) to him. 'But yesterday you did not teach them to me thus', he protested. 'Must you then not rely upon me? Then rely upon me with respect to the Oral (Torah) too.'

On another occasion it happened that a certain non-Jew came before Shammai and said to him, 'Make me a proselyte, on condition that you teach me the whole Torah while I stand on one foot.' Thereupon he repulsed him with the builder's cubit which was in his hand. When he went before Hillel, he said to him, 'What is hateful to you, do not do to your neighbour: that is the whole Torah, while the rest is the commentary (*pirushah*) thereof; go and learn it [lit. 'perfect it'].'

On another occasion it happened that a certain heathen was passing behind a Bet haMidrash, when he heard the voice of a *sopher* reciting, 'And these are the vestments they shall make; a breastpiece, an ephod' [Ex. xxviii.4]. Said he, 'For whom are these?' 'For the high priest', he was told. Then said that heathen to himself, 'I will go and become a proselyte, that I may be appointed a high priest.' So he went before Shammai and said to him, 'Make me a proselyte on condition that you appoint me a high priest.' But he repulsed him with the builder's cubit which was in his hand. He then went before Hillel, who made him a proselyte. He said to him, 'Can any man be made a king but he who knows the arts of government? Go and study the arts of government.' He went and read. When he came to, 'Any unqualified person who comes near it shall be put to death' [Num. i.51], he asked him, 'To whom does this verse apply?' 'Even to David King of Israel', was the answer. Thereupon that proselyte reasoned within himself by *qal waḥomer*: if Israel, who are called sons of the Omnipresent, and who in his love for them he designated them, 'Israel is my son, my firstborn', yet it is written of them, 'Any unqualified person who comes near it shall be put to death'; how much more so a mere proselyte, who comes with his staff and wallet. Then he went before Shammai and said to him, 'Am I then eligible to be a high priest? Is it not written in the Torah, "Any unqualified person who comes near it shall be put to death"?' He went before Hillel and said to him, 'O gentle Hillel, blessings rest on your head for bringing me under the wings of the Shechinah.' Some time later the three met in one place; they said: 'Shammai's impatience sought to drive us from the world, but Hillel's gentleness brought us under the wings of the Shechinah.'

4.7 Shab. 108a

Our Rabbis taught: *Tephillin* can be written upon the skin of clean animals and upon the skin of clean beasts, and upon the skin of animals improperly killed, or those blemished or diseased [lit. *nebeloth wterephoth*], and they are tied round with their hair, and sewn with their tendons. And it is a *halakah* from Moses at Sinai that *tephillin* are tied round with their hair and sewn with their tendons. But we may not write (them) upon the skin of unclean animals or upon the skin of unclean beasts, and the skin of the *nebeloth* and *terephoth* need not be stated (as unfit) nor may they be tied round with their hair or sewn with their tendons. And this question a certain Boethusian asked R. Joshua haGarsi: 'How do we know that *tephillin* may not be written upon the skin of an unclean animal?' Because it is written, 'that the law of the Lord may be always on your lips'[Ex. xiii.9], (implying) of that which is permitted in your mouth. If so, they should not be written on the skin of *nebeloth* and *terephoth*? He said to him: 'I will give you a comparison. What does this resemble? Two men who were condemned to death by the State, one being executed by the king and the other by the executioner. Who stands higher? Surely he who was slain by the king!' [And *nebeloth* and *terephoth* are slain by God.] 'If so let them be eaten?' 'Torah says, "You shall not eat any *nebelah*" [Dt. xiv.21]', he retorted, 'yet you say, let them be eaten.' 'Well spoken!' admitted he.

4.8 Erub. 13b

R. Abba stated in the name of Samuel: 'For three years there was a dispute between Bet Shammai and Bet Hillel, the former asserting, "The *halakah* is in agreement with our views," and the latter contending, "The *halakah* is in agreement with our views." Then a *bath qol* issued announcing, "(The utterances of) both are the words of the living God, but the *halakah* is in agreement with the rulings of Bet Hillel." ' Since, however, both are 'the words of the living God', what was it that entitled Bet Hillel to have the *halakah* fixed in agreement with their rulings? Because they were kindly and modest, they studied their own rulings and those of Bet Shammai, and were even so (humble) as to mention the actions of Bet Shammai before theirs.

For examples of issues between Bet Hillel and Bet Shammai, see the Index under Bet Hillel. With this passage, cf. also 5.13.

4.9 Pes. 57a

It was of these (men of violence) and of such as these that Abba Saul b. Batnith said in the name of Abba Joseph b. Ḥanin,

'Woe is me because of the house of Boethus,
Woe is me because of their clubs,
Woe is me because of the house of Hanin,
Woe is me because of their whisperings,
Woe is me because of the house of Kathros,
Woe is me because of their pens,
Woe is me because of the house of Ishmael b. Phiabi,
Woe is me because of their fists,
For they are high priests,

Their sons are treasurers,
Their sons-in-law officers of law
Their servants beat people with clubs.'

4.10 Pes. 70b

It was taught: Judah the son of Durtai separated himself (√*prsh*), he and his son Durtai, and went and dwelt in the South. He said: 'If Elijah should come and say to Israel, "Why did you not sacrifice the *ḥagigah* on the Sabbath?", what can they answer him? I am astonished at the two greatest men of our generation, Shemaiah and Abtalyon, who are great Ḥakamim and great interpreters (*drshin*), yet they have not told Israel. The *ḥagigah* over-rides the Sabbath.' Rab said, 'What is the reason of the son of Durtai? Because it is written, "You shall sacrifice the Passover offering to the Lord your God from the flock and from the herd" [Deut. xvi.2]; yet surely the Passover offering is only from lambs or goats? But "flock" refers to the Passover offering, (while) "herd" refers to the *ḥagigah*, and the Divine Law says, "And you shall sacrifice the Passover offering." ' Said R. Ashi: 'And are we to arise and explain the reason of the *prushim*?'

4.11 Yoma 2a

We learned in this case [M.Yom. i.1]: seven days before the burning of the Red Heifer the priest who was to burn the heifer was removed from his house to the cell in the north-eastern corner before the Temple [lit. *birah*, from I Chron. xxix.1]. It was called the cell of the stone chamber. And why was it called the cell of the stone chamber? Because all its functions (in connection with the Red Heifer) had to be performed only in vessels made of either pebbles, stone or earthenware. What was the reason? Since a *tebul yom* was permitted to (perform the ceremony of) the heifer, as we have learnt, they rendered the priest ritually impure to remove (a false notion) from the minds of the Sadducees, who used to say: 'Only by those on whom the sun has set could it be performed.' The

Rabbis ordained that only vessels made of pebbles, stone, or earthenware – which are immune to impurity – should be used in connection with the heifer, lest the ceremony thereof be treated slightly.

Cf. 2.31 *and the further references.*

4.12 Yoma 19b

'He turned aside (√*prsh*) and wept and they turned aside and wept': he turned aside and wept because they suspected him of being a Sadducee, and they turned aside and wept, for R. Joshua b. Levi said 'Whosoever suspects good folks will suffer (for it) on his own body.' Why was all this necessary? Lest he arrange the incense outside and thus bring it in, in the manner of the Sadducees.

Our Rabbis taught: There was a Sadducee who had arranged the incense without, and then brought it inside. As he left he was exceedingly glad. On his coming out his father met him and said to him: 'My son, although we are Sadducees, we are afraid of the *prushim.*' He replied: 'All my life I was aggrieved because of this Scripture verse: "For I appear in the cloud above the cover" [Lev. xvi.2]. I would say: When shall the opportunity come to my hand so that I might fulfil it? Now that such opportunity has come to my hand, should I not have fulfilled it?' It is reported that it took only a few days until he died and was thrown on the dungheap and worms came forth from his nose. Some say: He was smitten as he came out (of the Holy of Holies). For R. Ḥiyya taught: 'Some sort of a noise was heard in the Temple Court, for an angel had come and struck him down on his face (to the ground) and his brethren the priests came in and they found the trace as of a calf's foot on his shoulder, as it is written: "Their legs were straight, and their hooves were like the hooves of a calf" [Ezek. i.7].'

Cf. 2.11 *and the further references.*

4.13 Yoma 53a

Our Rabbis taught: 'And he shall put the incense on the fire before the Lord' [Lev. xvi.13], i.e., he must not put it in order outside and thus bring it in. (This is) to remove the error from the minds of the Sadducees who said: He must prepare it without, and bring it in. What is their interpretation? 'For I appear in the cloud above the cover' [Lev. xvi.2]: that teaches us that he prepares it outside and brings it in. The Ḥakamim said to them: 'But it is said also, "And he shall put the incense on the fire before the Lord" [Lev. xvi.13].' If so for what purpose then is it stated 'For I appear in the cloud above the cover'? It comes to teach us that he puts into it a smoke-raiser. Whence do we know that he must put a smoke-raiser into it? Because it is said: 'So that the cloud of the incense may cover the ark-cover.'

Cf. 2.11 *and the further references.*

4.14 Sukk. 43b

The rite of the *lulab* over-rides the Sabbath at the beginning, and that of the willow-branch at the end. On one occasion the seventh day of the (ceremonial of the) willow-branch fell on a Sabbath, and they brought saplings of willows on the Sabbath eve and placed them in the courtyard of the Temple. The Boethusians, having discovered them, took and hid them under some stones. On the morrow some of the *'amme haAreẓ* discovered them and removed them from under the stones, and the priests brought them in and fixed them in the sides of the altar. (The reason for hiding the willows was that) the Boethusians do not admit that the beating of the willow-branch over-rides the Sabbath.

Cf. 3.5 *and the further references.*

4.15 Sukk. 48b, 49a

Our Rabbis taught: It once happened that a certain Sadducee poured the water libation over his feet and all the people pelted him with their *ethrogim*. On that day the horn of the altar became damaged, and a handful of salt was brought and it was stopped up, not because the altar was thereby rendered valid for the service, but merely in order that it should not appear damaged, for an altar which has not the ascent, the horn, the base and the square shape is invalid for the service. R. Jose b. Judah adds, 'Also the circuit.'

Cf. 1.3 *and the further references.*

4.16 R.H. 18b

It has been said: Rab and R. Ḥanina said that *Megillath Ta'anith* has been annulled; R. Joḥanan and R. Joshua b. Levi hold that the *Megillath Ta'anith* has not been annulled, interpreting the words of the prophet [Zech. viii.19] thus: 'When there is peace, these days shall be for joy and gladness, but when there is no peace, they shall be fasts', and placing the days mentioned in the *Megillath Ta'anith* on the same footing. R. Joḥanan and Joshua b. Levi hold that the *Megillath Ta'anith* has not been annulled, maintaining that it was those others (mentioned by the prophet) that the All-Merciful made dependent on the existence of the Temple, but these (mentioned in *Megillath Ta'anith*) remain unaffected.

R. Kahana cited the following in objection: 'On one occasion a fast was decreed in Lydda on Ḥanukah [mentioned in *Meg. Ta'an.*] and R. Eliezer went down there and bathed and R. Joshua had his hair cut and they said to the inhabitants, "Go and fast in atonement for having fasted (on this day)." ' R. Joseph said 'Ḥanukah is different, because there is a religious ceremony (attached to it).' Abaye said to him: 'Is it then to be abolished and its ceremony with it (because it is not commanded in Scripture)?' R. Joseph thereupon (corrected himself and) said: 'Ḥanukah is different because it commemorates publicly a miracle.'

R. Aḥa b. Huna raised an objection: 'On the third of Tishri the mention (of God) in bonds was abolished', for the Grecian government [lit. 'kingdom of Javan'] had forbidden the mention of the name of heaven by the Israelites, and when the government of the Hasmonaeans became strong and defeated them, they ordained that they should mention the name of God even on bonds, and they used to write thus: 'In the year So-and-so of Joḥanan, High Priest to the Most High God', and when the Ḥakamim heard of it they said, 'Tomorrow this man will pay his debt and the bond will be found lying thrown away.' So they stopped them, and they made that day a feast day. Now if you maintain that *Megillath Ta'anith* has been annulled, (is it possible that) while the former (prohibitions of fasting) have been annulled, new ones should be added? With what are we here dealing? With the period when the Temple was still standing. But (if that is so), cannot the prohibition (of the third of Tishri) be derived from the fact that it was the day on which Gedaliah the son of Ahikam was killed? Rab replied: 'Its (insertion in *Megillath Ta'anith*) was required only to prohibit the day before it also.' But the prohibition of the day before it can also be derived from the fact that it is the day after New Moon? New Moon is ordained by the Written Law, and the ordinances of the Written Law do not require reinforcement, as it has been taught: 'These days which are mentioned in *Megillath Ta'anith* are forbidden (for fasting on), along with both the day before them and the day after them.' As to Sabbaths and New Moons, they themselves are forbidden, but the days before and after them are permitted. What is the difference between one set and the other? The one set are ordained by Torah, and the words of Torah require no re-inforcement, whereas the other are laid down by the scribes, and the words of the scribes (*dibre sopherim*) require reinforcement. But cannot the prohibition (of the second of Tishri) be derived from the fact that it is the day before the day on which Gedaliah the son of Ahikam was killed? R. Ashi replied: 'The fast of Gedaliah the son of Ahikam is laid down in the *dibre qabbalah* (later parts of Scripture, Prophets and Writings) and the words of the later Scriptures are on the same footing as those of the Torah.'

. . . There is a difference of opinion between Tannaim (as to whether the *Megillath Ta'anith* has been annulled), as it has been taught: 'These days which are mentioned in the *Megillath Ta'anith* are prohibited (to be kept as fast days) whether in the period when the Temple is standing or in the period when the Temple is not standing.' So R. Meir. R. Jose says: 'In the period when the Temple is standing they are prohibited, because they (Israel) have cause for rejoicing; in the period when the Temple is not standing they are permitted, because they have cause for mourning.' The law is that these prohibitions are annulled and the law is that they are not annulled. There is a contradiction, is there not, between these two laws? There is no contradiction: the one (prohibiting fasting) relates to Ḥanukah and Purim, the other to the other days.

For Joḥanan, see 7.6, *and the further references in* 1.2. *On the 'words of the scribes', see* 2.24 *and the further references.*

4.17 R.H. 22b

Our Rabbis taught: What evil course did the Boethusians adopt? Once the Boethusians sought to mislead the Ḥakamim. They hired two men for four hundred *zuzim*, one belonging to our party (*mshlnu*) and one to theirs. The one of their party gave his evidence and departed. Our man (came and) they said to him: 'Tell us how you saw the moon.' He replied: 'I was going up the ascent of Adumim and I saw it couched between two rocks, its head like (that of) a calf, its ears like (those of) a hind, and its tail lying between its legs, and as I caught sight of it I got a fright and fell backwards, and if you do not believe me, why, I have two hundred *zuzim* tied up in my cloak.' They said to him: 'Who told you to say all this?' He replied: 'I heard that the Boethusians were seeking to mislead the Ḥakamim, so I said, I will go myself and tell them, for fear lest untrustworthy men should come and mislead the Ḥakamim.' They said: 'You can have the two hundred *zuzim* as a present, and the man who hired you shall be laid out on the post.' There and then they ordained that testimony should be received only from persons who were known to them.

Cf. 2.14 *and the further references.*

4.18 Ḥag. 16b

Our Rabbis taught: The three of the former *zugoth* who said that the laying on of hands may not be performed, and the two of the latter pairs who said that it may be performed, were *nasi* [lit. *nesi'im*], and the others were *ab* (*aboth*) *bet din*. This is the view of R. Meir. But the Ḥakamim say: Judah b. Tabbai was *ab bet din*, and Simeon b. Shetaḥ was *nasi*. Who taught the following teaching of our Rabbis? Judah b. Tabbai said :'May I see Consolation, if I did not have a false witness put to death in order to remove from the heart of the Sadducees their saying that false witnesses were not to be put to death unless the accused had already been put to death.' Simeon b. Shetaḥ said to him: 'May I see the Consolation, if you did not shed innocent blood.' For the Ḥakamim said: 'False witnesses are not put to death until the two of them have been proved false, and they are not ordered to pay damages until the two of them have been proved false.' At this Judah b. Tabbai undertook never to give a decision except in the presence of Simeon b. Shetaḥ. All his days Judah b. Tabbai prostrated himself on the grave of the executed man, and his voice used to be heard. The people believed that it was the voice of the executed man. He said to them: 'It is my voice. You shall know this when on the morrow after I die my voice will not be heard.' R. Aḥa b. Raba said to R. Ashi: 'But perhaps he appeased him, or he (the deceased) summoned him to judgement.' According to whom will this be? Granted that if you say with R. Meir that Simeon b. Shetaḥ was *ab bet din* and Judah b. Tabbai was *nasi*, that is why he decided points of law in the presence of Simeon b. Shetaḥ. But if you say with the Rabbis that Judah b. Tabbai was *ab bet din* and Simeon b. Shetaḥ was *nasi*, how may the *ab bet din* decide points of law in the presence of the *nasi*? In fact his undertaking was with reference to association: I will not even join (with the other judges).

Cf. 2.25 *and the further references for the dispute about the treatment of false witnesses. For the laying on of hands, see* 2.16 *and the further reference.*

4.19 Ḥag. 23a

'Vessels that have been finished in purity': Who finished them? Should one say that a *ḥaber* finished them, then why do they require immersion? If, on the other hand, an *'am haAreẓ* finished them, can they be called 'finished in purity'? Rabbah b. Shila said that R. Mattenah said that Samuel said: 'Actually, (one can say) that a *ḥaber* finished them, yet (the vessel requires immersion) lest the spittle of an *'am haAreẓ* (fell upon it).' When could it have fallen (upon it)? Should one say, before he finished it, then it is not yet a vessel. If, on the other hand, after he had finished it, then he would surely take good care of them. Actually, (one can say that it fell upon it) before he finished it, but perhaps at the time when he finished it, it was still moist. (It states:) It requires (only) immersion, but not sunset: our Mishnah, therefore, is not according to R. Eliezer. For we have learnt: If a (reed) pipe [M.Kel. xviii.7] was cut for (putting therein ashes of) purification, R. Eliezer says: 'It must be immersed forthwith.' R. Joshua says: 'It must (first) be rendered unclean, and then immersed.' Now we raised the point: Who could have cut it? Should one say that a *ḥaber* cut it, then why is immersion required? If, on the other hand, an *'am haAreẓ* cut it, how can R. Joshua, in such a case, say: 'It must (first) be rendered unclean, and then immersed?' Behold, it is already unclean. Now Rabbah b. Shila said that R. Mattenah said that Samuel said: 'Actually, (you can say) that a *ḥaber* cut it, yet (immersion is required) lest the spittle of an *'am haAreẓ* (fell upon it).' (Again) when could it have fallen (upon it)? Should one say before he cut it, then it is not yet a vessel. If, on the other hand, after he had cut it, he would surely take good care of it. Actually, (you can say that it fell on the vessel) before he cut it, but perhaps at the time that he cut it, it was still moist. Granted (then) according to R. Joshua, a distinction is thus made, (as a demonstration) against the Sadducees. For we have learnt: They used to render the priest that was to burn the (Red) Heifer unclean, as a demonstration against the view of the Sadducees, who used to say: 'It must be performed (only) by those on whom the sun has set.' But according to R. Eliezer, granted if you say that in all other cases we do require sunset, a distinction is thus made (as a demonstration) against the Sadducees, but if you say that in other cases (too) we do not require sunset, what distinction is there, (as a demonstration) against the Sadducees? (Hence R. Eliezer cannot be right).

For the Red Heifer, see 2.31 *and the further references. On the* 'amme haAreẓ, *see especially* 4.22 *(beginning) and the Index.*

4.20 Ket. 62b

Rabbah, son of R. Hanan said to Abaye: 'How is it with an ass-driver who becomes a camel-driver (and is thus absent from home longer; must he ask his wife?)?' He replied: 'A woman desires one *qab* and enjoyment more than nine *qabim* and *prishut*.'

4.21 Sot. 15a

It has been taught: Rn. Gamaliel said to the Ḥakamim: 'O scribes (*sopherim*), let me explain this allegorically (*kmyn ḥmr*) . . .'

4.22 B.Sot. 22a,b

Our Rabbis taught: Who is an *'am haAreẓ*? Whoever does not recite the *Shema'* morning and evening with its accompanying benedictions. So according to R. Meir. The Ḥakamim say, 'Whoever does not put on *tephillin*.' Ben Azzai says, 'Whoever has not the fringe upon his garment.' R. Jonathan b. Joseph says, 'Whoever has sons and does not rear them to study Torah.' Others say, 'Even if he learnt Scripture and Mishnah but did not attend upon Rabbinical scholars, he is an *'am haAreẓ*. If he learnt scripture but not Mishnah, he is a boor (*bor*); if he learnt neither Scripture nor Mishnah, concerning him Scripture declares, "I will sow Israel and Judah with the seed of man and the seed of cattle" [Jer. xxxi.27].'

'My son, fear the Lord and the king, and mingle not with them that are given to change' [Prov. xxiv.21: 'given to change' is *shonim*, suggesting, therefore, a connection with Mishnah and with *shonim*, the transmitters of tradition]. R. Isaac said: 'They are the men who learn legal decisions' (*shonim halakoth*). This is self-evident: (It is not, because) you might have supposed (that the text meant), 'they who repeat a sin', and that it is according to the teaching of R. Huna; for R. Huna said: 'When a man commits a transgression and repeats it, it becomes to him something which is permissible.' Therefore he informs us (that this is not the intention of the text). A Tanna taught: 'The Tannaim (who transmit decisions) bring destruction upon the world.' How can it occur to you to say that they bring destruction upon the world? Rabina said: 'Because they decide points of law from their teachings (without the reasoning which leads up to them).' It has been similarly taught: R. Joshua said: 'Do they destroy the world? Rather do they cultivate the world, as it is said, "As for the ways, the world is for him" [Hab. iii.6, a literal reproduction of the text, *halakoth 'olam lo*: see B.Meg. 28b].' But (the reference is to) those who decide points of law from their teachings.

'A female *prushah*, etc.': Our Rabbis have taught: A maiden who gives herself up to prayer, a gadabout widow, and a minor whose months are not completed, behold these bring destruction upon the world. But it is not so; for R. Joḥanan has said: 'We learnt fear of sin from a maiden (who gave herself up to prayer) and (confidence in) the bestowal of reward from a (gadabout) widow.' Fear of sin from a maiden, for R. Joḥanan heard a maiden fall upon her face and exclaim, 'Lord of the Universe! You have created Paradise and Gehinnom. You have created righteous and wicked. May it be your will that men should not stumble through me.' (Confidence in) the bestowal of reward from a widow: a certain widow had a synagogue in her neighbourhood; yet she used to come daily to the School of R. Joḥanan and pray there. He said to her, 'My daughter, is there not a synagogue in your neighbourhood?' She answered him, 'Rabbi, but have I not the reward for the steps?' When it is said (that they bring destruction upon the world) the reference is to such a person as Joḥani the daughter of Retibi. What means 'a minor whose months are not completed'? They explained it thus: 'It refers to a disciple who rebels against the authority of his teachers.' R. Abba said: 'It refers to a disciple who has not attained the qualification to decide questions of law and yet decides them'; for R. Abbahu declared that R. Huna said in the name of Rab: 'What means that which is written, "Many she has pierced and laid low, and her victims are without number" [Prov. vii.26]?' 'Many she has pierced [i.e., wounded]': this refers to a disciple who has not attained the qualifications to decide questions of law and yet decides them; 'yea, all her slain are a mighty host': this refers to a disciple who has attained the qualification to decide questions of law and does not decide them. At what age (is he qualified)? At forty. But it is not so, for Rabbah decided questions of law. (He did so only in a town where the Rabbis) were his equals.

'And the wounds of the *prushim*, etc.': Our Rabbis taught: There are seven types of *prushim*: the *shikmi prush*, the *niqphi prush*, the *qizai prush*, the 'pestle' *prush*, the prush (who constantly exclaims) 'What is my duty that I may perform it?', the *prush* from love and the *prush* from fear. The *shikmi prush*: he is one who performs the action of Shechem. The *niqphi prush*: he is one who knocks his feet together. The *qizai prush*: R. Naḥman b. Isaac said: 'He is one who makes his blood to flow against walls.' The 'pestle' *prush*: Rabbah b. Shila said: '(His head) is bowed like (a pestle in) a mortar.' The *prush* (who constantly exclaims) 'What is my duty that I may perform it?' – but that is a virtue! No, what he says is, 'What further duty is there for me that I may perform it?' The *prush* from love and the *prush* from fear: Abaye and Raba said to the tanna (who was reciting this passage); 'Do not mention "the *prush* from love and the *prush* from fear"; for Rab Judah has said in the name of Rab: "A man should always engage himself in Torah and the commandments even though it be not for their own sake, because from (engaging in them) not for their own sake, he will come (to engage in them) for their own sake."' R. Naḥman b. Isaac said: 'What is hidden is hidden, and what is revealed is revealed; the Great Tribunal will exact punishment from those who rub themselves against the walls.'

King Jannai said to his wife, 'Fear not the *prushim* and the non-*prushim* but the hypocrites (*ẓbw'in*) who ape the *prushim*; because their deeds are the deeds of Zimri but they expect a reward like Phineas.'

> *For the advice of Jannaeus, cf.* 1.4. *On* makkot perushim, *see* 2.21 *and the further reference. On the seven types of* perushim, *see* 5.3, 6.3. *For references to* 'am(me) haAreẓ, *see the Index* ad loc.; *and for an example of attacks on the* 'amme haAreẓ, *see especially B.Pes.* 49*a*,*b*.

4.23 Sot. 48a

It has been taught: He (Joḥanan the high priest) also annulled the confession and decreed (*gzr*) in respect of *demai*, because he sent (inspectors) throughout the Israelite territory and discovered that they only separated (√*prsh*) the great *terumah* but as for the first and second tithes some fulfilled the law while others did not. So he said to (the people), 'My sons, come, I will tell you this. Just as in (the neglect) of the "great *terumah*" there is mortal sin, so with (the neglect) to present the *terumah* of the tithe and with the use of untithed produce there is mortal sin.' He thus arose and decreed for them that whoever purchases fruits from an *'am haAreẓ* must separate the first and second tithes therefrom. From the first tithe he separates the *terumah* of the tithe and gives it to a priest, and as for the second tithe he should go up and eat it in Jerusalem. With regard to the first tithe and the tithe of the poor, whoever demands them from his neighbour has the onus of proving (that they had not been already apportioned). (Joḥanan) made two decrees: he abolished the confession (over the presentation of the first tithe) in the case of the Ḥaberim and decreed in regard to the *demai* of the *'amme haAreẓ*. 'He also abolished the Awakeners': What does 'Awakeners' mean? Reḥabah said: 'The Levites used daily to stand upon the dais and exclaim, "Awake, why do you sleep, O Lord?" [Ps. xliv.24]. He said to them, 'Does, then, the All-Present sleep? Has it not been stated, "The guardian of Israel never slumbers, never sleeps" [Ps. cxxi.4]?' But so long as Israel abides in trouble and the Gentiles are in peace and comfort, the words 'Awake, why do you sleep, O Lord?' (should be uttered). 'And Stunners': What does 'Stunners' mean? Rab Judah said in the name of Samuel: 'They used to make an incision on the calf between its horns so that the blood should flow into its eyes. (Joḥanan) came and abolished the practice because it appeared as though (the animal had) a blemish.' There is a *baraitha* which teaches: They used to strike (the animal) with clubs as is the practice with idolatry. (Joḥanan) said to them, 'How long will you feed the altar with *nebeloth*?' (How could he have described the carcasses as) *nebeloth* when they had been properly slaughtered? Rather (should they be described as) *terefoth*, since the membrane of the brain may have been perforated. He (thereupon) arose and ordained rings for them in the ground. 'Up to his days the hammer used to strike in Jerusalem': On the intermediate days of the Festival. 'All his days there was no need to enquire about *demai*': As we have explained above.

Cf. 1.2 *and the further references.*

4.24 Qid. 43a

When it was taught that if a man says to his agent, 'Go and kill some person', the agent is culpable but the man who sent him is not, Shammai the Elder said in the name of Haggai the prophet: 'The man who sent him is culpable, because it is said: "You murdered by the sword of the Ammonites" [II Sam. xii.9].'

4.25 Qid. 66a

It once happened that King Jannai went to Koḥalith in the wilderness and conquered sixty towns there. On his return he rejoiced exceedingly and invited all the Ḥakamim of Israel. He said to them: 'Our forefathers ate mallows when they were engaged on the building of the (second) Temple; let us too eat mallows in memory of our forefathers.' So mallows were served on golden tables, and they ate. Now, there was a man there, frivolous, evil-hearted and worthless, named Eleazar son of Poʿirah, who said to King Jannai: 'O King Jannai, the hearts of the *prushim* are against you.' 'Then what shall I do?' 'Test them by the plate between your eyes.' So he tested them by the plate between his eyes. Now an elder, named Judah son of Gedidiah, was present there. He said to King Jannai: 'O King Jannai, let the royal crown suffice you, and leave the priestly crown to the seed of Aaron.' (For it was rumoured that his mother had been taken captive in Modiʿim.) Accordingly, the charge was investigated, but not sustained, and the Ḥakamim of Israel departed in anger. Then said Eleazar b. Poʿirah to King Jannai: 'O King Jannai, that is the law even for the most humble man in Israel, and you, a king and a high priest, shall that be your law (too)?' 'Then what shall I do?' 'If you will take my advice, trample them down.' 'But what shall happen with the Torah?' 'Behold, it is rolled up and lying in the corner: whoever wishes to study, let him go and study.' Said R. Naḥman b. Isaac: 'Immediately a spirit of heresy (*epiqorsoth*) was instilled into him, for he should have replied, "That is well for the Written Law, but what of the Oral Law?" ' Straightway the evil burst forth through Eleazar son of Poʿirah, all the Ḥakamim of Israel were massacred, and the world was desolate until Simeon b. Shetaḥ came and restored the Torah to its pristine (glory). Now, how was it? Shall we say that two testified that she was captured and two that she was not? What (reason) do you see to rely upon the latter or rely upon the former? Hence it must surely mean (that her captivity was attested) by one witness, and the reason (that his evidence was rejected) was that two rebutted him; but otherwise, he would have been believed. And Raba? (He will reply:) 'After all, there were two against two, but it is as R. Aḥa b. R. Manyomi said (elsewhere): that it refers to witnesses of refutation; so here too, there were witnesses of refutation.' Alternatively, this agrees with R. Isaac, who said: 'They substituted a bondmaid for her.'

Cf. 1.2 *and the further references.*

4.26 B.B. 60b

Our Rabbis taught: When the Temple was destroyed for the second time, *prushim* increased in Israel, binding themselves neither to eat meat nor to drink wine. R. Joshua got into conversation with them and said to them: 'My sons, why do you not eat meat nor drink wine?' They replied: 'Shall we eat flesh which used to be brought as an offering on the altar, now that this altar is in abeyance? Shall we drink wine which used to be poured as a libation on the altar, but now no longer?' He said to them: 'If that is so, we should not eat bread either, because the meal offerings have ceased.' They said: 'We can manage with fruit.' 'We should not eat fruit either, because there is no longer an offering of first-fruits.' 'Then we can manage with other fruits.' 'But we should not drink water because there is no longer any ceremony of the pouring of water.' To this they could find no answer, so he said to them: 'My sons, come and listen to me. Not to mourn at all is impossible, because the blow has fallen. To mourn overmuch is also impossible, because we do not impose on the community a hardship which the majority cannot endure, as it is written, "There is a curse, a curse on you all, the whole nation of you, because you defraud me" [Mal. iii.9]. The Ḥakamim therefore have ordained thus: "A man may stucco his house, but he should leave a little bare" '. . . It has been taught: R. Ishmael ben Elisha said: 'Since the day of the destruction of the Temple we should by rights bind ourselves not to eat meat nor drink wine, only we do not lay a hardship on the community unless the majority can endure it. And from the day that a government has come into power which issues cruel decrees against us and forbids to us the observance of the Torah and the precepts and does not allow us to enter into the "week of the son" [according to another version, "the salvation of the son"], we ought by rights to bind ourselves not to marry and beget children, and the seed of Abraham our father would come to an end of itself. However, let Israel go their way: it is better that they should err in ignorance than presumptuously.'

Cf. 3.11.

4.27 B.B. 115b

R. Huna said in the name of Rab: 'Anyone, even a prince (*nasi*) in Israel, who says that a daughter is to inherit with the daughter of the son, must not be obeyed; for such (a ruling) is only the practice of the Sadducees.' As it was taught: On the twenty-fourth of Tebeth we returned to our (own) law; for the Sadducees having maintained (that) a daughter inherited with the daughter of the son, Rn. Joḥanan b. Zakkai joined issue with them. He said to them: 'Fools, whence do you derive this?' And there was no one who could reply a word, except one old man who prated at him and said: 'If the daughter of his son, who succeeds (to an inheritance) by virtue of his son's right, is heir to him, how much more so his daughter who derives her right from himself?' He (Joḥanan) read for him this verse, 'These are the sons of Seir the Horite, the original inhabitants of the land: Lotan, Shobal, Zibeon, Anah' [Gen. xxxvi.20]; and (lower down) it is written, 'These are the sons of Zibeon: Aiah and Anah' [Gen. xxxvi.24; therefore, Anah is both brother and son of Zibeon, so brother and son must have equal rights of inheritance]. (But this) teaches that Zibeon had intercourse with his mother and begat Anah. Is it not possible that there were two (called) Anah? Rabbah said: . . . 'Scripture says: "This is Anah", (implying): the same Anah that was (mentioned) before.' He said to him: 'O, master, do you dismiss me with such (a feeble reply)? [If Anah is a *son* there is no dispute: the Sadducees accept the principle where *sons* are concerned].' He said to him: 'Fool, shall not our perfect Torah be as (convincing) as your idle talk! [Anah was a *daughter* and did not inherit as the sister of the deceased, but as granddaughter of Seir.] (Your deduction is fallacious, for) the reason why a son's daughter (has a right of inheritance is) because her claim is valid where there are brothers, but can the same be said of the (deceased's) daughter whose right (of inheritance) is impaired where there are brothers?' Thus they were defeated. And that day was declared a festive day.

Cf. 3.19 *and the further reference.*

4.28 San. 19a,b

But why this prohibition of the kings of Israel? Because of an incident which happened with a slave of King Jannai, who killed a man. Simeon b. Shetaḥ said to the Ḥakamim: 'Set your eyes boldly upon him and let us judge him.' So they sent the king word, saying: 'Your slave has killed a man.' Thereupon he sent him to them (to be tried). But they again sent him a message 'You too must come here, for the Torah says, "If the owner has been duly warned" [Ex. xxi.29], (teaching) that the owner of the ox must come and stand by his ox.' The king accordingly came and sat down. Then Simeon b. Shetaḥ said: 'Stand on your feet, King Jannai, and let the witnesses testify against you; yet it is not before us that you stand, but before him who spoke and the world came into being, as it is written, "Then both the men between whom the controversy is, shall stand, etc." [Dt. xix.17].' 'I shall not act in accordance with what you say, but in accordance with what your colleagues say', he answered. [19b] (Simeon) then turned first to the right and then to the left, but they all (for fear of the king) looked down at the ground. Then said Simeon b. Shetaḥ to them: 'Are you wrapped in thoughts? Let the Master of thoughts (God) come and call you to account.' Instantly, Gabriel came and smote them to the ground, and they died. It was there and then enacted: A king (not of the House of David) may neither judge nor be judged; neither testify, nor be testified against.

> *Cf.* 1.6 *and the further references. For a summary of the discussion of the identity of the two incidents, see A. Guttmann,* Rabbinic Judaism, *pp.* 50*f.*

4.29 San. 33b

'But not for condemnation, etc.': R. Ḥiyya b. Abba said in the name of R. Joḥanan: 'Providing that he erred in a matter which the Sadducees do not admit. But if he erred in a matter which even they admit, let him go back to school and learn it.'

> *Cf.* 4.32

4.30 San. 52b

R. Eliezer b. Ẓadok said: 'It once happened that a priest's daughter committed adultery', etc.: R. Joseph said: 'It was a Sadducee Bet Din that did this.' Now, is this what R. Eliezer b. Ẓadok said, and did the Ḥakamim answer him so? Has it not been taught: R. Eliezer b. Ẓadok said: 'I remember, when I was a child riding on my father's shoulder, that a priest's adulterous daughter was brought (to the place of execution), surrounded by faggots, and burnt.' The Ḥakamim answered him: 'You were then a minor, whose testimony is inadmissible.' There were two such incidents. Now which incident did he first relate to them? Shall we say that he first told them of the incident first mentioned here (which happened in his majority): but if he told them what happened in his majority, and they paid no attention to him, surely he would not proceed to tell them what occurred in his minority? But he must have related this one (of the Baraitha) first, to which they replied: 'You were a minor.' Then he told them of the case that occurred in his majority, and they replied, 'That was done because the Bet Din at that time was not learned in the law.'

Cf. 2.23 *and the further references.*

4.31 A.Z. 20b

R. Phineḥas b. Jair said: 'Torah leads to strict observance, strict observance leads to heedfulness, heedfulness leads to cleanliness, cleanliness leads to *prishut*, *prishut* leads to purity, purity leads (to saintliness, saintliness leads) to humility, humility leads to the shunning of sin, the shunning of sin leads (to holiness (*qdwshah*), holiness leads) to the holy spirit, the holy spirit leads to the resurrection of the dead'; and saintliness (*ḥsidwth*) is greater than all these, as it is said: 'Then you spoke in vision to your holy ones (*lehasideka*)' [Ps. lxxxix.19 (20)].

Cf. 2.22 *(end).*

4.32 Hor. 4a

Rab Judah said in the name of Samuel: 'The court is liable for giving an (erroneous) ruling only in the case of a prohibition which the Sadducees do not admit, but if concerning a prohibition which the Sadducees admit they are exempt. Why? It is a matter which anyone can learn at school.'

Cf. 4.29.

4.33 Makk. 5b

It is taught: BeRibbi put the principle of the mishnah in this way: if they (the false witnesses) have not caused death they are put to death; if they have caused death, they are not put to death . . . It has been taught: R. Judah b. Tabbai said: 'May I see Consolation if I did not have one false witness done to death to disabuse the mind of the Sadducees, who used to say that false witnesses (found guilty) were put to death only after the (falsely) accused person had (actually) been executed.' Said Simeon b. Shetaḥ to him: 'May I see Consolation if you have not shed innocent blood because the Ḥakamim declared that witnesses found to be false are not put to death until both have been proved as such, and are not (juridically) flogged until both have been proved as such.' Forthwith Judah b. Tabbai resolved never to deliver a decision save in the presence of Simeon b. Shetaḥ. And all through his (remaining) days, Judah b. Tabbai used to go and prostrate himself on the grave of that (executed) witness, and his voice would be heard, and people thought it was the voice of the slain man; but he would tell them, 'It is my voice. You will be convinced when on the morrow of my own [lit. 'this man's'] death, his voice will be heard no more.' R. Aḥa son of Raba said to R. Ashi: 'He might perhaps have answered the summons of the deceased, or else he might have obtained his forgiveness.'

Cf. 2.25 *and the further references.*

4.34 Zeb. 21a

In the case of the Red Heifer we defile the high priest, for we learnt, they used to defile the priest who was to burn the heifer and then make him immerse, in order to combat the opinion of the Sadducees, who maintained: the ceremony was performed only by those on whom the sun had set. This proves that uncleanness does not invalidate it. (But) the Red Heifer is different, because a man in a state of suspended uncleanness (*tebul yom*) is not unfit for it. If so, why must he purify himself (at all)? Because we want it equal (in terms of respect) to (the usual) sacrificial offering.

Cf. 2.31 *and the further references.*

4.35 Men. 65a,b

Our Rabbis taught: On the following days fasting, and on some of them also mourning, is forbidden: from the first until the eighth day of the month of Nisan, during which time the Daily Offering was established, mourning is forbidden; from the eighth of the same until the close of the Festival, during which time the date for the feast of Weeks was re-established, fasting is forbidden. 'From the first until the eighth day of the month of Nisan, during which time the Daily Offering was established, mourning is forbidden.' For the Sadducees used to say that an individual may of his own free will defray the cost of the Daily Offering. What was their argument? It is written, 'The one lamb you shall sacrifice in the morning and the second between dusk and dark' [Num. xxviii.4]. And what was the reply? It is written, 'See that you present my offerings, the food for the food-offering of soothing odour, to me at the appointed time' [Num. xxviii.2]. Hence all sacrifices were to be taken out of the Temple fund.

From the eighth of the same until the close of the Festival (of Passover), during which time the date for the feast of Weeks was re-established, fasting is forbidden. For the Boethusians held that the feast of Weeks must always be on the day after the Sabbath. But Rn. Joḥanan b. Zakkai entered into discussion with them saying, 'Fools that you are, whence do you derive it?' Not one of them was able to answer him, save one old man who commenced to babble and said, 'Moses our teacher was a great lover of Israel, and knowing full well that the feast of Weeks lasted only one day he therefore fixed it on the day after the Sabbath so that Israel might enjoy themselves for two successive days.' (Rn. Joḥanan b. Zakkai) then quoted to him the following verse, ' "The journey from Horeb through the hill-country of Seir to Kadesh-Barnea takes eleven days" [Deut. i.2]. If Moses was a great lover of Israel, why then did he detain them in the wilderness for forty years?' 'Master', said the other, 'is it thus that you would dismiss me?' 'Fool', he answered, 'should not our perfect Torah be as convincing as your idle talk?' Now one verse says, 'You shall number fifty days', [Lev. xxiii.16], while the other verse says, 'Seven full weeks' [Lev. xxiii.15]. How are they to be reconciled? The latter verse refers to the time when the (first day of the) Festival (of Passover) falls on the Sabbath, while the former to the time when the (first day of the) Festival falls on a weekday.

On paying for Tamid, see 7.1. *For the feast of Weeks, cf.* 2.17 *(*4*).*

4.36 Bek. 30b

Our Rabbis taught: If one is prepared to accept the obligation of a *ḥaber* (*dbre ḥbirwth*) except for one religious law, we must not receive him (as a *ḥaber*). If a heathen (star-worshipper) is prepared to accept the Torah except one religious law, we must not receive him (as an Israelite). R. Jose son of R. Judah says: 'Even (if the exception be) one point of the special minutiae of the scribes' enactments (*dqdwq 'ḥd mdbre sopherim*).' And similarly if a son of a Levite was prepared to accept the duties of the community of Levites except one religious law, we must not receive him (as a Levite). If a priest was prepared to accept the duties of the priesthood except one religious law, we must not receive him (as a priest), as it is said, 'He (among the sons of Aaron) who presents the blood, etc.' [Lev. vii.33], implying the (entire) service that is transmitted to the sons of Aaron and that any priest who does not acknowledge this has no share in (the privileges of) the priesthood.

Our Rabbis taught: If one applies to become a *ḥaber* (*dbre ḥbirwth*), if we saw him practising these privately at his house, we receive him and subsequently instruct him, but if not, we first instruct him and then receive him (as a *ḥaber*). But Simeon b. Yoḥai says: 'Both in the first case and the second, we receive him (as a *ḥaber*) and he learns incidentally as he goes on.' Our Rabbis taught: We accept a *ḥaber* if he promises to observe cleanness of hands and afterwards we accept him as one who will observe the other rules of levitical purity. If he said: 'I only promise to observe cleanness of hands', we receive him (as a *ḥaber*, as his promise is important in connection with levitical purity). If, however, he promised to observe the rules of levitical purity but not cleanness of hands, then even his promise to observe the rules of levitical purity is not regarded as a genuine promise.

Our Rabbis taught: How long is the period before we receive him (as a *ḥaber*)? Bet Shammai say: 'As regards (the purity of his) liquids (whose uncleanness is of a light character), the period is thirty days, but as regards the purity of (his) garment, the period is twelve months.' But Bet Hillel say: 'Both in the one case as well as in the other, the period is twelve months.' If this is so, then you have here a ruling where Bet Shammai is more lenient and Bet Hillel is the stricter? Rather (read): Bet Hillel say: 'Both in the one case as well as in the other, the period is thirty days.' (Mnemonic: A *Ḥaber*, Scholar, Purple-blue, Repent, Tax-collector.) Our Rabbis taught: One who desires to accept the obligations of a *ḥaber* is required to do so in the presence of three *ḥaberim*, whereas his sons and the members of his family are not required to accept (these obligations) in the presence of three *ḥaberim*. But R. Simeon b. Gamaliel says: 'His sons and the members of his family are also required to accept (these obligations) in the presence of three *ḥaberim*, because the case of a *ḥaber* who accepts (these obligations) is not on a par with the case of the son of a *ḥaber* who accepts (them).'

Our Rabbis taught: One who desires to accept the obligations of a *ḥaber* is required to accept them in the presence of three *ḥaberim* and even a *talmid ḥakam* (a scholar) is required to accept the obligations in the presence of three *ḥaberim*. An elder, a member of a scholars' council (*yshibah*), is not required to accept (these obligations) in the presence of three *ḥaberim*, having already accepted them from the time when he took his place at the council. Abba Saul says: 'Even a *talmid ḥakam* is not required to accept the obligations of a *ḥaber* in the presence of three *ḥaberim*. And not only this, but even others may accept the obligations of a *ḥaber* in his presence.' Said R. Joḥanan: 'In the days of the son of R. Ḥanina b. Antigonus was this teaching taught. For R. Judah and R. Jose were in doubt concerning a matter of levitical cleanness. They sent a pair of scholars to the son of R. Ḥanina b. Antigonus. They went and asked him to enquire into the matter. They found him carrying levitically prepared food. He seated some of his own disciples with them, while he stood up to look in to the question. They came and informed R. Judah and R. Jose (of his conduct towards them). R. Judah said to them: "His father held scholars in contempt and he also holds scholars in contempt." R. Jose replied to him: "Let the dignity of the elder lie undisturbed in its place, but from the day that the Temple was destroyed, the priests guarded their dignity by not entrusting matters of levitical cleanness to everybody." ' Our Rabbis taught: (The wife of a *ḥaber* is considered as a *ḥaber*). If a *ḥaber* dies, his wife and the members of the family retain their status until there is reason to suspect them. And similarly a court-yard in which *tekeleth* (purple-blue) was sold retains its status until it is disqualified. Our Rabbis taught: The wife of an *'am haAreẓ* who was married to a *ḥaber*, likewise a daughter of an *'am haAreẓ* who was married to a *ḥaber*, and similarly the slave of an *'am haAreẓ* who was sold to a *ḥaber*, all of these must first accept the obligations of a *ḥaber*. But the wife of a *ḥaber* who was married to an *'am haAreẓ*, likewise the daughter of a *ḥaber* who was married to an *'am haAreẓ*, and similarly the slave of a *ḥaber* who was sold to an *'am haAreẓ*, need not first accept the obligations of a *ḥaber*. R. Simeon b. Eliezer says: 'Even the latter require first to accept the obligations of a *ḥaber*.' For R. Simeon b. Eliezer reported in the name of R. Meir: 'It happened with a certain woman who was married to a *ḥaber* that she fastened the straps of the *tephillin* on his hand and when afterwards married to a publican, she knotted the custom seals for him.'

Cf. 2.2 *and the further references.*

4.37 Nidd. 33b, 34a

Our Rabbis taught: It once happened that a Sadducee was conversing with a high priest in the market place when some spittle was squirted from his mouth and fell on the clothes of the high priest. The face of the high priest turned yellow and he hurried to his wife, and she said to him that although they were wives of Sadducees they paid homage to the *prushim* and showed their blood to the Ḥakamim. R. Jose observed: 'We know them better than anybody else (and can testify) that they show their menstrual blood to the Ḥakamim. There was only one exception, a woman who lived in our neighbourhood who did not show her blood to the Ḥakamim, but she died.' But why was he not concerned about the uncleanness that is occasioned by the spittle of an *'am haAreẓ*? Abaye replied: 'This was a case of a Sadducee who was a *ḥaber.*' Raba said: 'Is a Sadducee who is a *ḥaber* presumed to have intercourse with a menstruant?' 'Rather', said Raba. The incident occurred during a festival and the uncleanness of an *'am haAreẓ* during a festival the Rabbis treated as clean; for it is written, 'So all the men of Israel were gathered against the city, knit together (*ḥaberim*) as one man' [Jud. xx.11]. The text thus treated them all as *ḥaberim.*

Cf. 3.17 *(3).*

PALESTINIAN TALMUD

5.1 Ber. i.4

The Ḥaberim say in the name of R. Joḥanan: 'The words of the scribes (*dibre sopherim*) are related to the words of Torah and are to be loved like the words of Torah . . .' R. Ishmael said: 'The words of Torah include both prohibitions and permissions; they include commands both of light and weighty importance, but the words of the scribes (*dibre sopherim*) are all weighty. This can be known from the saying, "He who says that there should be no *tephillin*, thereby contradicting Torah, is without guilt, but (he who says) there should be five compartments, thereby adding to the words of the scribes (*dibre sopherim*) is guilty." ' R. Ḥananiah b. R. Ada said in the name of R. Tanḥum b. R. Hiyya: 'The words of the elders (*dibre zeqenim*) are weightier than the words of the prophets, as it is written: "Prophesy not, who prophesy: they shall not prophesy to them, these insults are their own invention" [Mic. ii.6]; then it is written: "I will prophesy to you of wine and strong drink" [Mic. ii.11].'

The latter part also appears in J.San. x.3 *where M.San.* xi.3 *has* dibre sopherim *for* dibre zeqenim. *A further passage from J.Ber.* i.4 *appears in J.Yeb.* i.6 *(*5.13*). On the 'words of the scribes', see* 2.24 *and the further references.*

5.2 Ber. ii.4

It is taught: all which pertains to the *minim* and to the wicked (*rsh'im*) is in the (section of the *Shemoneh 'Esreh*) 'abasement of the evil', and what pertains to proselytes and elders is in the 'confidence for the righteous', and what pertains to David is in the 'building of Jerusalem'.

Cf. 3.1.

5.3 Ber. ix.5

There are seven types of *prushim*: the *shikmi prush*; the *niqphi prush*; the *qizai prush*; the *prush* (who says), 'What is my (self-)

denial?'; the *prush* who says, 'If I know my guilt, I will compensate'; the *prush* who fears; the *prush* who loves. The *shikmi prush*: he carries the commandments on his shoulders. The *niqphi prush*: spare me a moment and I will fulfil my obligation. The *qizai prush*: in enacting this sin and this command, the one will balance the other. The *prush* (who says), 'What is my (self-) denial?': from the little that belongs to me I will give up some to fulfil a command. The *prush* who says, 'If I know my sin I will compensate: tell me the sin I have done, and I will fulfil an equal obligation.' The *prush* who fears: like Job. The *prush* who loves: like Abraham. Our father Abraham made the evil inclination good, as it is written, 'And you found his heart faithful before you' [Neh. ix.8].

The same passage is recorded in J.Sot. v.5. *On the seven types, see* 4.22 *and the further reference.*

5.4 Ber. ix.5 (end)

R. Simeon b. Laqish said: 'In the *Megillath Ḥasidim* can be found written, "If you abandon me for one day I will abandon you for two." It is like two men who set out, one from Tiberias, the other from Sepphoris, and who met each other in a certain inn. They then proceeded to separate (*lprwsh*) again and went, the first a *mil* and the second also a *mil*, until there was to be found separating them two *milin*.'

5.5 Dem. ii.3

It is taught: everyone who comes (to become a *ḥaber*) must take on himself the obligations [commentators add, 'in the presence of three *ḥaberim*'] even if he is a trained scholar (*talmid ḥakam*). But the Ḥakam who has sat in the assembly (*yshibah*) has no need to take on himself the obligations because he has already taken them on himself at the time of joining the assembly. R. Ila said: 'Even he (must do so) who took them on himself on the earlier occasion.' R. Jose objected: 'In that case, what is the distinction between a Ḥakam and an *'am haAreẓ*?' The opinion of R. Ila accords with Resh Laqish: when Resh Laqish was joining those of the house of R. Jannai, the people recognised him and fled from his presence. He said to them: 'I come to your house as an *'am haAreẓ* in matters of cleanness.' It is taught: he (the head of the household) makes his vow to the *ḥaburah*, and his sons and the sons of his household make their vow to him. Elsewhere it is taught: he and his sons and the sons of his household make their vow to the *ḥaburah*. There is no conflict: the first applies to those who are still dependent on their fathers, the second to those who are not. According to R. Ḥalafta b. Saul: 'Those of age make their vow to the *ḥaburah*, minors make it to him.' It is taught: initially he undertakes cleanness of hands and then proceeds to cleannesses in general. R. Isaac b. R. Eleazar said: 'Cleanness of hands, uncleanness by indirect contact, uncleanness caused by *hesset* (shaking), uncleannesses (especially in relation to food), tithes: (this is the sequence).'

Cf. 2.2 *and the further references.*

5.6 Shebi. i.5

R. Zeira in the name of R. (I)la, R. Jose in the name of R. Joḥanan, said: 'The willow branch (carried round the altar during Sukkot) is a *halakah* going back to Moses from Sinai.' This is not so according to Abba Saul; he said, 'The willow branch is a command of Torah, "... and willows [plural] from the riverside" [Lev. xxiii.40]: there is one branch for the *lulab* and another for the temple.' R. Aba and R. Hiyya in the name of R. Joḥanan: 'The willow branch and the water libation are *halakoth* going back to Moses from Sinai.' This is not so according to R. Aqiba; he said: 'The water libation is a command of Torah, "On the second day . . . and their drink offering [Num. xxix.17,19], . . . on the sixth day . . . and its drink offerings [Num. xxix.29,30], . . . on the seventh day . . . as prescribed according to their number" [Num. xxix.32,33].' The additional (Hebrew) letters make *maim* (waters). . . . R. Aba b. Zabdi in the name of R. Hunya of the valley of Ḥiwra [Sukk.: Brath Ḥawran/Ḥoran]: 'The willow branch, the water libation, and the young trees (with reference to the sabbatical year) are derived from the former [Sukk. om. 'former'] prophets.'

The same, with slight variants, occurs in J.Sukk. iv.1. *For the willow branches, see* 3.5 *and the further references. For the water libation, see* 1.3 *and the further references.*

5.7 M.Sh. ii.10

These are the judges: ben Azzai and ben Zoma; these are the *talmidim*: Ḥanina b. Ḥakinai and R. Eleazar b. Matia; the holy community (*'dah qdwshah*): R. Jose b. haMeshullam and R. Simeon b. Menasia.

On the holy community, see 6.8.

5.8 Yoma i.5

'He turned aside (√*prsh*) and wept': because he was put to shame; 'they turned aside (√*prsh*) and wept': because they had to do this. And why the adjuring? Because of the Boethusians, who used to say, 'He should prepare the incense on the outside and take it within.' It happened that a certain one of them prepared the incense outside and took it within, and when he came out, he said to his father: 'Although you and your fellows have been interpreters all your days, you have not enacted it until this man (myself) stood up and enacted it.' He replied: 'Although we have been interpreters all our lives, nevertheless we act according to the precepts (*krẓwn*) of the Ḥakamim. I will be astonished if this man lives much longer.' They said: 'Very few days went by before he was dead.' Others say, 'He died with worms coming out of his nose . . .' It is said to be the same one (who acted wrongly) in the case of the Red Heifer, Sukkah and the Day of Atonement. R. Simon did not say so, but rather that it is one man in the case of the Red Heifer and Sukkah, and another in the case of the Day of Atonement; or one in the case of the Red Heifer and the Day of Atonement, and another in the case of Sukkah (hence the two different deaths).

The latter part ('it is said to be . . .') appears in J.Sukk. iv.6. *Cf.* 2.11 *and the further references for the Day of Atonement. For the Red Heifer, see* 2.31 *and the further references. For Sukkah, see* 3.5 *and the further references.*

5.9 Sheq. v.1

R. Eleazer said: 'To Ezra, the priest and scribe, a scribe' [Ezra vii.11]: what is the repetition of *sopher* (scribe) except to indicate that as he was a scribe with respect to the words of (*bdbre*) Torah' so he was a scribe with respect to the words of the Ḥakamim.

Cf. 3.13 *and the further reference.*

5.10 R.H. ii.1

It happened once that the Boethusians hired two false witnesses to bear witness that the new moon had been properly observed. The one came and gave his witness and departed, the other came and said: 'I was going up the ascent of Adumim and I saw it couched between two rocks, its head like that of a calf, its ears like those of a hind, and I saw it and I was terrified and drew back, and here are two hundred *zuzim* folded in my purse.' . . .

Cf. 2.14 *and the further references.*

5.11 Ḥag. ii.2

We have learnt: Judah b. Tabbai was *nasi* and Simeon b. Shetaḥ was *ab bet din*. But we have also learnt the opposite. In support of the claim that Judah b. Tabbai was *nasi* one can cite the matter of Alexandria: the people of Jerusalem wished to confer on Judah b. Tabbai the office of *nasi* in Jerusalem, but he fled to Alexandria; and the people of Jerusalem used to write: 'From Jerusalem the great to Alexandria the small, how long will my beloved [lit. 'betrothed'] dwell with you, since I now dwell prevented from marrying!'

For references to Simeon b. Shetaḥ and Judah b. Tabbai, see the Index.

5.12 Ḥag. iii.8

Once it happened that they were immersing the *menorah*; the Sadducees said: 'Look, the *prushim* are immersing the orb of the sun!,

Cf. 3.9.

5.13 Yeb. i.6 (end)

If a man follows the light rulings, first of one, then of the other [i.e., of Bet Shammai and Bet Hillel], he is called wicked: it must be either according to the words of Bet Shammai, light and severe, or according to the words of Bet Hillel, light and severe. This applies to the period before the coming forth of the *bath qol*. But after the *bath qol*, *halakah* was established for ever according to the words of Bet Hillel; and anyone who transgresses the words of Bet Hillel is liable to death. It is taught: 'The *bath qol* came forth and said: "(These words are) both words of the living God, but *halakah* is according to Bet Hillel for ever." ' When did the *bath qol* come forth? Rab Bibi said in the name of R. Joḥanan: 'The *bath qol* came forth in Yavneh.'

The latter part also appears in J.Ber. i.4 *(7). With this passage, cf.* 4.8. *This passage also immediately precedes the section of Sot.* iii.4, *translated in* 5.14.

5.14 Sot. iii.4

'A woman *prushah*': This is the one who sits down to study and reads an improper meaning into the words of Torah, such as 'She (Leah) said to him, "You are to sleep with me tonight . . ." That night he slept with her' [Gen. xxx.16]. R. Abbahu said: '(The words were) only formed in her mind, as it were'; he himself knew what came into her mind, that it was in order to establish the tribes. 'The blows (*makkot*) of the *prushim*': this is the one who gives advice to orphans to take from the allotted portion of the widow (their mother). Thus the widow of R. Shubtai was squandering the estate. The orphans went to R. Eleazer for advice. He said to them: 'Fools! There is nothing I can do for you: repay the *ketubah* [the repayment of which dissolves the widow's claim on the estate].' Another (who heard this) said: 'I will tell you what to do: make out that you are selling the estate, and she will claim the endowment and lose her right to be supported (from the estate).' They put the deceit into practice, but she came that evening (when she discovered it) to R. Eleazer. He said: 'Here is one whom the *makkot prushim* have assailed. May evil come upon me if I intended this to happen to her.' A certain pupil of Rabbi had two hundred *denarii* all but one [i.e., 199, which entitled him to receive the tithe of the poor]. Rabbi used to give him, every third year, the tithe of the poor. On one occasion the other pupils regarded him jealously and they (gave him one *zuz* and) brought him up to the total. When Rabbi wished to help him just as he used to, he said to him, 'Rabbi, I have the legal amount [lit. 'sufficiency'].' He said: 'Here is one whom the *makkot prushim* have assailed.' He hinted this to the pupils, who went to an inn and made him a single *qarat* poorer [because he bought them drinks], and Rabbi helped him again just as he used to.

> *The second incident is also recorded in J.Peah* viii.8. *On* makkot prushim, *see* 2.21 *and the further reference. For the immediately preceding passage, see* 5.13.

5.15 Ket. viii.11

Simeon b. Shetaḥ decreed three things: a man may do business with his wife's *ketubah*; young children must go to the *bet sepher* [elementary school]; and he decreed that uncleanness attaches to vessels of glass.

> *Cf.* 4.4 *and the further reference.*

5.16 B.B. viii.1

The Sadducees say: 'The daughter of a son and the daughter are both equal', and their argument is as follows: as the daughter of the (my) son who is directly descended from my son inherits from me, surely my daughter who is descended directly from myself ought legally to inherit from me. They said to them: 'Not so: if you admit (our argument, as you do) that the daughter of the son only inherits by virtue of (her father's relation to) the brothers, then you will agree that the daughter could only inherit by virtue of (her relation to) the grandfather.'

> *Cf.* 3.19 *and the further references.*

5.17 San. x.5

R. Joḥanan said: 'Israel was not exiled until twenty four sects of heretics (*minim*) were brought into being. What is the force of, "Man, I am sending you to the Israelites, rebellious nations who have rebelled against me" [Ezek. ii.3]? Scripture does not say "to the rebellious nation", but "to the rebellious nations [i.e. the Hebrew text has the plural], who have rebelled against me". They and their fathers have sinned against me to this day [cf. Ezek. ii.3].'

OTHER RABBINIC WORKS

6.1 A.R.N.A. v. (Schechter 13b)

Antigonus of Socho took over from Simeon the Just. He used to say: 'Be not like slaves who serve their masters for the sake of compensation; be rather like slaves who serve their master without thought of compensation, and let the fear of heaven be upon you, so that your reward may be doubled in the age to come.' [N.B. the clause at the end, which does not appear in P.A. i.3 (2.26).]

Antigonus of Socho had two disciples (*talmidim*) who used to study his words. They taught them to their disciples, and their disciples to their disciples. These proceeded to examine the words closely and asked: 'Why did our ancestors see fit to say this thing? Is it possible that a labourer should do his work all day and not take his reward in the evening? If our ancestors, in fact, had known that there is another world and that there will be a resurrection of the dead, they would not have spoken in this manner.'

So they arose and withdrew from Torah (*pirshu min haTorah*) and split into two sects, the Sadducees and the Boethusians: Sadducees named after Zadok, Boethusians, after Boethus. And they used silver vessels and gold vessels all their lives – not because they were ostentatious; but the Sadducees said, 'It is a tradition amongst the *prushim* to afflict themselves in this world; yet in the world to come they will have nothing.'

See also 6.2; *on the house of Boethus, see* 4.9.

6.2 A.R.N.B. *ibid.*

Antigonus of Socho had two disciples, Zadok and Boethus. They heard this word and repeated it (*shnu*) to their disciples. And their disciples spoke the word from their master (*rabban*) without its interpretation (*pirusho*). They said to them: 'If you had known that there will be a resurrection of the dead and a reward of the righteous in the age to come, you [lit. 'they'] would not have spoken in this manner.' So they became apostates (*hlbu*) and separated (*pirshu*), and there arose from them two families, the Sadducees (named after Zadok), and the Boethusians named after Boethus.

See also 6.1.

6.3 A.R.N. xxxvii.4

There are eight [corrd. by commentators to 'seven'] types of *prushim*: the *shikmi prush*; the *niqphi prush*; the *prush* who bleeds; the pestle (or 'mortar') *prush*; the *prush* who has his duty; the *prush* who says . . . [untranslatable: commentators, 'What is my duty and I will do it?']; the *prush* from . . . [untranslatable]; the *prush* from fear.

Cf. 4.22 *and the further reference.*

6.4 Vay.R. xxiv.4

The Holy One, blessed be he, said to Moses: 'Go and say to the children of Israel: "My children: as I am *prush*, so you also, be *prushim*; as I am holy (*qdwsh*), so you also, be holy (*qdwshim*)": Speak to all the community of the Israelites in these words: "You shall be holy, because I, the Lord your God, am holy" [Lev. xix.2].'

Cf. 6.9; 6.11; 6.12; 6.13; 6.14.

6.5 Vay.R. xxxv.10

It happened in the days of Simeon ben Shetaḥ and in the days of Salome the queen that rain used to fall on Sabbath nights, until wheat grew as large as kidneys, barley as large as olives, lentils as large as gold denarii. The Ḥakamim gathered some of them and left them for future generations. Why was that? To make known what are the results of sin, in accord with what is said: 'Your wrongdoing has upset nature's order, and your sins have kept from you her kindly gifts' [Jer. v.25].

For Salome, see 1.4 *and the further references.*

6.6 Bem.R. ix.16

It is the custom for the daughters of Israel to have their heads covered. Therefore, when the priest uncovers the hair of her head [Num. v.18], he says to her: 'You have separated (*prsht*) from the custom of the daughters of Israel whose custom is to have their head covered, and you have walked in the ways of the nations (*goyim*) who walk with their heads uncovered: here, then, is what you wanted.'

6.7 Bem.R. x.1

As a man separates himself (*pwrsh 'th 'ẓmw*) from the fruit of *'orlah* (growth of the first three years), so will those who become entangled with handmaids be separated (*prushim*) from the righteous on the day of judgement.

6.8 Qoh.R. ix.9.1

Rabbi said in the name of the holy community: 'Take up work for yourself as well as Torah . . .' Why does he say 'holy community'? Because it included R. Jose b. Meshullam and R. Simeon b. Menasia; they used to divide the day into three parts, one for Torah, one for prayer, one for work. Others say: they worked in Torah in the winter and in their work in the summer. R. Isaac b. Eliezer used to call R. Joshua b. R. Timi and R. Borqai 'a holy community', because they divided the day into three parts, one for Torah, one for prayer, one for work.

On the holy community, see 5.7.

6.9 Mekilta: On Ex. xix.6 (Baḥod. §2)

'Holy': holy and sanctified, separated (*qdwshim wmqwdshim prushim*) from the world and from their abominations.

Cf. 6.4.

6.10 On Ex. xxiii.6 (Kasp. §3)

Once Simeon b. Shetaḥ sentenced to death one false witness against whom an alibi had been established. Judah b. Tabbai then said to him: 'May I see the Consolation if you did not shed innocent blood. For the Torah said: You may sentence to death on the evidence of witnesses, and also, you may sentence witnesses to death on the basis of an alibi. Just as there must be two witnesses giving evidence, so also must there be two against whom an alibi is established.' And once Judah b. Tabbai entered a ruin and found a slain man still writhing, and a sword still dripping blood was in the hand of the apparent slayer. Said Judah b. Tabbai to him: 'May . . . come upon me, if it be not true that either I or you killed him. However, what can I do, since Torah has said, "At the mouth of two witnesses . . ." [Dt. xix.15]? But he who knows all, even the thoughts of man, will exact punishment of that man.' Hardly had he come out, when a serpent bit that man, and he died.

Cf. 2.25 *and the further references.*

6.11 Mekilta deR. Simeon b. Yohai: On Ex. xix.6 (Hoffmann p. 95)

'You are a holy nation to the Lord your God': this means sanctification through the commandments: for when the Holy One, blessed be he, adds a new command to Israel, he adds a further (opportunity for) sanctification.

Cf. 6.4.

6.12 Sifra: On Lev. xi.44 (Weiss 57b)

'For I am the Lord your God: you shall sanctify yourselves and be holy, for I am holy': even as I am holy (*qdwsh*), so you also shall be holy: even as I am *prush*, so you also shall be *prushim*.

See also Sifra on Lev. xi.45, xix.1*f.* *(Weiss* 86*c).* *Cf.* 6.4.

6.13 On Lev. xx.7 (Weiss 91d)

'You shall sanctify yourselves and be holy': this means the sanctification which consists in separation (*prshut*) from the heathen [lit. 'star-worshippers']. It is nothing other than the sanctification which consists in observing all the commandments, as it says, 'You shall be holy.'

Cf. 6.4.

6.14 On Lev. xx.26 (Weiss 93d)

'As I am holy, you also shall be (holy)': as I am *prush*, so you also shall be *prushim*. If you are separated (*'bdil*) from the nations you belong to me . . . but if you are not, then you belong to Nebuchadnezzar, the king of Babylon, and his companions (*ḥbiraw*).

Cf. 6.4.

6.15 Sifre. On Num. §112

R. Simeon b. Eliezer said: 'From this I have refuted the books/scribes of the Samaritans (*sphrey kuthay*) who say that the dead will not live. I said to them: it says, "That person shall be wholly cut off; the guilt shall be on his head alone" [Num. xv.31]. His iniquity could not be on him unless he were going to render his account (in the future) on the day of judgement.'

A different argument of R. Simeon b. Eliezer with the scribes of the Samaritans is recorded in J.Yeb. i.6 *(4).*

6.16 On Num. xviii.7 (§116)

'I bestow on you this gift of priestly service': to perform the eating of holy things (*qdshim*) in the country at large [i.e., those gifts which do not have to be consumed in Jerusalem] is like the service in the Temple: as the priest must sanctify his hands before service in the

Temple, so also he must sanctify his hands before eating holy things in the country . . . Rabbi said: 'To perform the eating of holy things is like the service in the Temple.' Does this obtain with the sanctifying of his hands and feet, (necessary) before the Temple service? . . . In the place where he needs both hands and feet he sanctifies both hands and feet, but in the place where he needs hands alone, he sanctifies only his hands. Hence we establish the washing of hands (before and after meals, *ntilth ydyim*) from Torah.

Cf. 2.17 *and the further references.*

6.17 On Dt. §323

Take upon yourselves the yoke of God's kingdom, give due place to one another, and deal with one another with acts of generous kindness (*gmilwth ḥsdim*).

Cf. 2.26 *(*2*). For the 'yoke of the kingdom', see* 4.1.

6.18 Tanḥ.B. i.159 (Vayeẓe 21)

The Holy One, blessed be he, knew what passed in his heart, and the Holy One, blessed be he, said to him: 'You seek that I should be with you: separate (*hprsh*) yourself from Laban the wicked, and I will be with you.'

6.19 Midrash Tehillim. On Ps. xv.1 (§3)

It is like a man from the country who visited the city. He saw all kinds of baked foods and delicacies on sale, and he asked: 'Can a man be fully satisfied with these?' His companion answered: 'Yes, if he has the money, and plenty of it.' So also David asked, 'Lord, who may lodge in your tabernacle?' The Holy One, blessed be he, said: 'He who obeys commandments, and plenty of them, and practises *prishut*.'

6.20 Sepher Yosippon (ed. Hominer, p. 112, ll. 16–19)

The *prushim* used to say: 'We keep the Torah which our fathers entrusted into our hands, interpreting (*mprshth*) it according to the Ḥakamim who interpreted (*prshu*) Torah traditionally (*lqblah*).' The Sadducees used to say: 'We do not adhere or listen to every tradition (*mswreth*) and every interpretation (*peyrush*), but to the Torah of Moses alone.'

6.21 Hekaloth Rabbati xviii

R. Ishmael said, 'At once I took a piece of woollen material (*prhba*) and gave it to R. Akiba, and R. Akiba gave it to a servant of ours, saying: "Go, and put this piece beside a woman who has immersed herself and is not yet entirely pure, and let her immerse herself (again). If that woman comes and testifies of her flow before the *ḥaburah*, there will be one who inhibits her (from her husband), but the majority will permit her. Say to that woman: 'Touch this piece with the tip of one finger, not pressing it hard, but like a man who removes an eyelash which has got into his eye, very gently.' " They went and did so, and put the material in front of R. Ishmael. He inserted a myrtle branch, oiled by being soaked in balsam, and they (thus) put it on the knees of R. Neḥuniah. At once they excluded him (*ptrwhw*) from (being) before the throne of glory where he was sitting and seeing

Wonderful heights and power extraordinary
Lifting up of exaltation and power of majesty –
Which comes to pass before the throne of glory
Three times in every day in the height
From the time when the world was created until now for praise.'

MEGILLATH TA'ANITH

7.1 On Nisan 1–8 (Lichtenstein, p. 323)

'From the first day of the month Nisan to the eighth, *tamid* was settled; mourning is forbidden': the gloss interprets the decision about *tamid* as the outcome of a dispute with the Boethusians. The Ḥakamim argue against them on the basis of Num. xxviii. 1f., in which *tamid* is set in the context of offerings which all Israel have to maintain.

Cf. 4.35.

7.2 On Nisan 8 to the end of the feast (Lich. p. 324)

'From the eighth to the end of the feast, the feast of Weeks was re-established; fasting and mourning are forbidden': the controversialists are again (according to the gloss) the Boethusians and the Ḥakamim. The commentator then adds a further discussion between 'a certain Boethusian and Joḥanan b. Zakkai'; it is the dispute in B.Men. 65a and further comments of R. Eliezer, R. Joshua, R. Ishmael and R. Judah b. Betheyra are also recorded.

Cf. 2.17 *and the further references.*

7.3 On Tammuz 14 (Lich. p. 331)

'On the fourteenth of Tammuz the book of decisions (*sepher gezeroth*) was abrogated': the gloss identifies three particular issues in which the decisions of the Sadducees differed from the arguments of the Ḥakamim. In the actual argument, the disputants are the Boethusians [Lich. 1.8]. The three issues are: interpretation of 'an eye for an eye'; the literal necessity for producing the stained garment as proof of virginity ('the words are as they are written'); and the meaning of *bephanaw* ('before him', or 'in his face') in the ritual of *ḥaliẓah*.

On lex talionis, *cf.* 2.25 *and the further references. On* ḥaliẓah, *cf.* 2.19.

7.4 On Ab 24 (Lich. p. 334)

'On the twenty-fourth we returned to our law (*ldinna*)': the gloss identifies the 'return to our law' with the Hasmonaean abolition of Greek courts; but the commentator adds a quite different interpretation: according to the commentator, the 'return to our law' commemorates the defeat of the Sadducees in their interpretation of the law of inheritance. The case against the Sadducees is argued by Rn. Joḥanan b. Zakkai.

Cf. 3.19 *and the further references.*

7.5 On Elul 22 (Lich. p. 336)

'On the twenty-second we returned to kill the apostates (*mshmdiya*)': the commentary gives examples of exemplary or deterrent punishments imposed by the Bet Din (or in one case by Simeon b. Shetaḥ), on the basis of the verse, 'All Israel shall hear of it and be afraid' (Dt. xiii.11).

7.6 On Tishri 3 (Lich. p. 337)

'On the third of Tishri, mention of the Divine name was removed from public deeds': it is the Ḥakamim who resist (successfully) the Hasmonaean attempt to write their names into public documents: 'They used to write as follows: "In the year so and so of Joḥanan the high priest, who is priest to El Elyon"' (cf. B.R.H. 18b).

For Joḥanan, cf. 1.2 *and the further references. Cf. also* 2.38 *(*8*). For the name of God in bonds, see* 4.16.

7.7 On Marḥeshvan 27 (Lich. p. 338)

'On the twenty-seventh the fine-flour offering began to be brought again to the altar': the gloss records a dispute between Joḥanan b. Zakkai and the Sadducees (not Boethusians):

'It is on account of the Sadducees who used to say that they could eat the meal-offering which goes with the animal sacrifice. Rn. Joḥanan b. Zakkai said to them, "What is your reason?" But they did not know how to answer from Torah, except for one who babbled against him and said: "Because Moses loved Aaron, he said: 'Do not eat meat alone, but eat meal and meat, like a man who says to his companion (*lḥbrw*), here is meat and here are delicacies.' " Rn. Joḥanan b. Zakkai recited to him: "They came to Elim, where there were twelve springs and seventy palm-trees, and there they encamped beside the water" [Ex. xv.27]. He answered: "What has that got to do with it?" He said: "Fool, do not let our perfect Torah (*torah shlmah*) be like your empty nonsense. Has it not already been said, 'They shall be a whole-offering to the Lord with the proper grain-offering and the proper drink-offering, a food-offering of soothing odour to the Lord' [Lev. xxiii.18; i.e., the *whole* offering is for the Lord]?" '

Cf. 2.28.

7.8 On Tebeth 28 (Lich. p. 342)

'On the twenty-eighth of Tebeth the assembly (*knshta*) was re-established according to law (*dina*)': the gloss records the story of Simeon b. Shetaḥ reasserting the presence of the *talmidim* in the Sanhedrin. According to the story, under Jannaeus and Salome the Sanhedrin was composed entirely of Sadducees, with the single exception of Simeon b. Shetaḥ. They attempted to reach decisions derived directly from Torah, and Simeon argued that anyone who could not do so should not be admitted as a member of the Court. There then came a case which they could not solve from Torah, but one old man asked for time to consider the matter; but having done so, he was still unable to offer a decision. Simeon then claimed that the Sanhedrin must consist of seventy-one members, and he replaced the old man with one of the *talmidim*. On this basis the Sanhedrin was eventually cleared of Sadducees.

Cf. 1.4 *and the further references.*

7.9 On Adar 17 (Lich. p. 347)

'On the seventeenth the people (*'mmiya*) rose against the remnant of the scribes (*pltth sphrya*) in the district of Cholqis in Bet Zabdi, and they were delivered': according to the gloss, this took place in the reign of Alexander Jannaeus: when he persecuted the Ḥakamim, they fled to Syria and settled in Cholqis. When the *goyim* attacked them, some of them took refuge in Bet Zabdi, from which they were eventually rescued.

Cf. 1.4 *and the further references.*

DEAD SEA SCROLLS

8.1 CDC iv.7–9

And all who come after them [8] (are) to act according to the interpretation of the law (*kepherush haTorah*) in which the first were instructed, until is completed [9] the time of these years.

8.2 CDC iv.19–21

The builders of the wall who walk (*haleku*) after 'precept' (*ẓav*) . . . [20] shall be taken in fornication twice, because they take [21] second wives while the first is still living, whereas the order of creation is, 'Male and female created he them' [Gen. i.27].

8.3 CDC v.6–12

And also they defile the Temple because they do not [7] make the distinction (*mabdil(im)*) according to Torah but lie with one who sees her discharge of blood. And they marry [8] each man the daughter of his brother or of his sister, though Moses said: 'To [9] your mother's sister you shall not approach: she is your mother's near kin' [Lev. xviii.13]. The law of incest for men [10] is written, but it applies also to women; so if the daughter of a brother uncovers the nakedness of the brother [11] of her father, she is his near kin. And also their holy spirit they defile, and with a tongue [12] full of blasphemy they open their mouth against the covenant of God, saying, 'We are not sure' (*lo nakonu*).

8.4 CDC v.20

At the time of the desolation of the land there arose removers of the boundary (*massigey haGebul*), and they led Israel astray.

8.5 CDC vi.14–21

They shall take care to act according to the interpretation of the law (*kepherush haTorah*) in the time of wickedness, and to be distinct from (*lehibbadel*) [15] the sons of the pit, and to avoid the unclean riches of wickedness belonging to vow (*neder*), ban (*ḥerem*) [16], or from the Temple treasure, and (to avoid) robbing the poor of his people, making widows their prey, [17] and the orphans their victims; and to distinguish (*lehabdil*) between clean and unclean, and to cause to be known the difference between [18] holy and unholy; and to keep the sabbath day according to its interpretation (*kepherushah*) and the feasts [19] and the day of fasting according to the ruling of the members of the New Covenant in the land of Damascus; [20] and to set aside the holy things according to their interpretations (*kepheyrusheyhem*); to love each man his brother [21] as himself; and to succour the poor, the needy and the stranger.

8.6 CDC xi.5–8

A man shall not go after his animal to pasture it outside the town more [6] than two thousand cubits. He shall not raise his hand to strike it with his fist. If [7] it is difficult he shall not take it out of his house. A man shall not take anything from his house [8] to the outside, nor from the outside into the house.

8.7 CDC xiii.4–6

And if [5] there is a judgement with respect to the law of leprosy (*mishpat latorath nega*ʿ) in a man's case, the priest shall come and stand in the camp, and there shall instruct him [6] the overseer (*haMabaqqer*) in the interpretation of the law (*beperush haTorah*) . . .

8.8 CDC xv.1

(He shall not swear) by *aleph* and *lamedh* [i.e. by El-ʾohim, by God], nor by *aleph* and *daleth* [i.e. by ʾA-donai, by the Lord], but rather he shall swear by the (covenant or) by the curses of the covenant;

[2] and the Torah of Moses he shall not mention, because . . . [3] and if he swears and breaks the oath, he profanes the Name.

8.9 IQH ii.13–16

You have set me up as a banner for the elect of righteousness (*ẓedeq*), and an interpreter (*meliẓ*) with the knowledge of wonderful mysteries as a test [14] for those who (seek after ?) truth, and as a standard for those who love correction (*musar*). I am a man of strife to those who interpret (*limeliẓey*) erroneously, (but a man of) [15] (peace) to all who see clearly. I am a spirit of zeal (*lruaḥ qin'ah*) towards all who seek smooth things (*dorshey ḥalaqoth*), [16] and all men of deceit (*anshe remiyah*) roar against me like the roar of many waters.

APOCRYPHAL WORKS

9.1 Ass.Mos. vi.1–2

Then will be raised up for them kings ruling and calling themselves Priests of the Most High God (*sacerdotes summi dei*), and they will do impious things in the Holy of Holies. And there will succeed them an insolent (*petulans*) king who will not be of the race of priests, a man over-bold and without shame, and he will judge them as they deserve.

9.2 Ass.Mos. vii.3–10

And, in the time of these, injuring and impious men will reign, who believe that they are just (*justos*). And these will rouse the wrath of their minds, being treacherous men, pleasing in their own sight, deceivers in all their works, and loving feasts at every hour of the day, devourers, gluttons . . ., (thieves) of the goods of the poor, saying that they do this out of pity, but destroyers of them, full of strife and deceit, concealing themselves lest they be recognised, impious, full of wickedness and evil from sunrise to sunset, saying, 'We will have feastings and luxury, eating and drinking, and we consider that we shall be as princes.' And though their hands and minds touch unclean things, and their mouth speaks proudly, and in addition they say, 'Touch me not lest you pollute me in the place . . .'

9.3 II Baruch xlii.4f.

As for those who were previously subject, but then withdrew and mixed themselves with the seed of mixed people, the (favoured) time of these was previously, and was reckoned as highly exalted.

As for those who previously had no knowledge, but then knew life, and mixed with the seed of those who separated themselves, the time of these is later and is reckoned as highly exalted.

9.4 IV Ezra xiv.18–26

I answered and said: 'Let me speak in your presence, Lord. I will indeed go as you have commanded and warn the people who are now alive. But what of those born later? Who will warn them?

The world is in darkness and its inhabitants are without light.

For your law is burnt, so that no one knows all that has been done by you, or all that you will yet do. If I have found favour with you, send in to me the Holy Spirit, that I may write all that has happened in the world from the beginning, the things written in your law, that men may be able to find the way, and that those who would live at the end may live.'

And he answered and said: 'Go and gather the people, and tell them not to seek you for forty days.

Get ready many writing tablets, and take with you Saraia, Dabria, Selemia, Elkanah, and Osiel, the five who are well-fitted for good writing.

And come here, so that I can light the lamp of understanding in your heart, which will not be put out until what you are going to write has been finished.

And when you have finished, part of it you must make public, but part you must give secretly to the wise.'

Cf. 3.13 *and the further reference.*

9.5 Oxyr. Pap. 840 (Grenfell and Hunt V, pp. 4ff.), l.7ff.

And he took them and brought them to the place of purification itself, and he was walking in the Temple. And a certain Pharisee (*pharisaios tis*), a chief priest, whose name was Levi, met them and said to the saviour: 'Who gave you permission to walk in this place of purifying (*agneuterion*), and to see these holy vessels, when you have not washed, nor have your disciples bathed their feet. But defiled, you have walked in this Temple which is a clean place, in which no other man walks unless he has washed himself and changed his clothes, and he does not look on these holy vessels.' And the saviour (stood) with his disciples (and said): 'Are you, then, being here in the Temple, clean?' He replied: 'I am clean, for I have washed in the pool of David, and having descended by one staircase

I have gone up by another, and I put on white and clean garments, and then I came and looked on these holy vessels.' The saviour answered him: 'Woe, you blind, who do not see: you have washed in these running waters in which dogs and pigs have been thrown night and day, and you have washed and wiped the surface of the skin, which prostitutes and flute girls anoint and wash and wipe and adorn for the lust of men. But within they are full of scorpions and evil. But I and (my disciples) whom you say have not bathed, have bathed in the waters of eternal life which come from . . .'

9.6 Gospel of Thomas §39

Jesus said: 'The Pharisees and the scribes have received the keys of knowledge but have concealed them. They did not go in themselves, nor did they allow others to go in who wished to do so. But as for you, be wise as serpents and innocent as doves.'

9.7 Acts of Thomas §102

Jesus said: 'Woe to the Pharisees who are like a dog sleeping in the manger of oxen: he does not eat himself, nor does he allow the oxen to eat.'

9.8 Clementine Homilies xi.28.4

Our teacher condemned some of the Pharisees and scribes among us (who are separate and, being scribes, know the law better than others), calling them hypocrites because they used to cleanse only what is visible to others, but ignored purity of heart, which is visible only to God.

The distinction among the Pharisees is then explained by the contrast between Mt. xxiii.2*f.* *and* 25*f.* *Cf. also Clementine Recognitions* i.54.

9.9 Origen: Commentary on Matthew xxiii.23

The Pharisees are all those who justify themselves, and who separate themselves from all others, saying, 'Do not come near me, for I am clean.' 'Pharisees' (from the name Phares) means 'separated', since they separate themselves from others. Phares means, in Hebrew, 'separation'.

For further patristic examples of a similar tradition, see E. Schurer, A History of the Jewish People, *Eng. tr., Edinburgh,* 1898, II.2, *pp.* 20*f.*

BIBLIOGRAPHY

The bibliography includes only those works to which specific reference is made in the Introduction or notes. In addition to the works listed, particular attention must be drawn to the article by A. Michel and J. le Moyne, 'Pharisiens', in *Supplément au Dictionnaire de la Bible*, VII, 1966, col. 1022–1115; and also to the introductory essay contributed by E. Rivkin to the reprint of W. Oesterley and H. Loewe, *Judaism and Christianity*, New York, 1969, pp. vii–lxx. The work by J. Neusner, on rabbinic traditions about the Pharisees before 70, appeared after this book had gone to the printer, otherwise more reference would have been made to its attempts to unravel the history of rabbinic traditions. The importance of this undertaking is immense, since otherwise generalisations about 'the worthwhileness of rabbinic evidence' will inevitably continue.

Allon, G., 'The Relation of the Perushim to the Authority of Rome and to the House of Herod', *Researches in the History of Israel*, Tel Aviv, 1957, pp. 26–47.

'The Application of the Halakoth on Purity', *loc. cit.* pp. 148–77.

Baeck, L., *The Pharisees*, New York, 1957.

Bammel, E., ed., *The Trial of Jesus*, London, 1970.

Baumgarten, J., 'Qumran Studies', *J.B.L.* LXXVII, 249–57.

Beilner, W., 'Der Ursprung des Pharisäismus', *B.Z.* III, 1959, 235–51.

Blinzler, J., see Bammel, E.

Bowker, J. W., *The Targums and Rabbinic Literature*, Cambridge, 1969.

'The Origin and Purpose of St John's Gospel'. *N.T.S.* XI, 398–408.

Catchpole, D. R., see Bammel, E.

Driver, G. R., *The Judaean Scrolls*, Oxford, 1965.

Feldmann, L., 'The Identity of Pollio, the Pharisee, in Josephus', *J.Q.R.* XLIX, 1958, 53–62.

Finkelstein, L., *The Pharisees*, Philadelphia, 1962.

HaPerushim weAnshe Keneset haGedolah, New York, 1950.

Geiger, A., *Nachgelassene Schriften*, Berlin, 1876.

Guttmann, A., 'Pharisaism in Transition', in *Essays in Honour of S. B. Freehof*, Pittsburgh, 1964.

Rabbinic Judaism in the Making, Detroit, 1970.

Hengel, M., 'Mk. vii.3, *pygme*: die Geschichte einer exegetischen Aporie und der Versuch ihrer Lösung', *Z.N.T.W.* IX, 1969, 182–98.

Hoenig, S. B., *The Great Sanhedrin*, New York, 1953.

Horbury, W., 'A Critical Examination of Toledoth Jeshu', unpubl. dissertation, Cambr. Univ. Library, 1971, Ph.D. 7422.

Jeremias, J., *Jesus' Promise to the Nations*, London, 1958.

Katsh, A. I., 'Unpublished Geniza Fragments of Pirke Aboth in the Antonin Geniza Collection in Leningrad', *J.Q.R.* LXI, 1970, 1–14.

Konowitz, I., *Bet Shammai – Bet Hillel: Collected Sayings in Halakah and Haggadah in Talmudic and Midrashic Literature*, Jerusalem, 1965.

Krauss, S. L., *Das Leben Jesu nach jüdischen Quellen*, Berlin, 1902.

Lauterbach, J. Z., 'The Sadducees and Pharisees', in *Studies in Jewish Literature: Issued in Honour of K. Kohler*, Berlin, 1913.

Liebermann, S., *The Tosefta and Tosefta Kifshuta*, New York, 1956, 1962.

Maimonides, M., *The Book of Judges*, trs. A. M. Hershman, Yale, 1949.

Mantel, H., *Studies in the History of the Sanhedrin*, Harvard (Semitic Series XVII), 1961.
'The Nature of the Great Synagogue', *H.T.R.* LX, 1967, 69–91.

Neusner, J., '*The Fellowship* (*Ḥaburah*) in the Second Jewish Commonwealth', *H.T.R.* LIII, 1960, 125–42.
The Rabbinic Traditions about the Pharisees before 70, Leiden, 1971.

Obermann, J. J., *The Arabic Original of ibn Shahin's* Book of Comfort, New Haven, 1933.

Reisel, M., *The Mysterious Name of Y.h.w.h.*, Assen, 1957.

Rivkin, E., 'Defining the Pharisees: the Tannaitic Sources', *H.U.C.A.* XL, 1969, 205–49.
'Pharisaism and the Crisis of the Individual in the Greco-Roman World', *J.Q.R.* LXI, 1970, 27–53.

Schurer, E., *A History of the Jewish People*, Eng. tr. Edinburgh, 1898.

Strack, H. L., *Jesus, die Häretiker und die Christen nach den ältesten jüdischen Angaben*, Leipzig, 1910.

Urbach, E. E., 'Class-Status and Leadership in the World of the Palestinian Sages', *Proc. I.A.S.H.* II, 1968, pp. 38–74.

Wieder, N., *The Judaean Scrolls and Karaism*, London, 1962.

Zeitlin, S., 'The Pharisees, a Historical Study', *J.Q.R.* LII, 1961, 97–129.
'The Origin of the Pharisees Reconsidered', *J.Q.R.* LIX, 1969, 255–67.
The Rise and Fall of the Jewish State, II, Philadelphia, 1967.

INDEX OF PASSAGES TRANSLATED

in alphabetical order where appropriate

4. Babylonian Talmud

5. Palestinian Talmud

6. Other rabbinic works

7. Megillath Ta'anith

8. Dead Sea Scrolls

9. Apocryphal works

INDEX OF REFERENCES TO THE TRANSLATED PASSAGES IN THE INTRODUCTION AND ADDITIONAL NOTE

INDEX OF REFERENCES

BIBLICAL

Old Testament

OTHER WRITINGS

RABBINIC WRITINGS

GENERAL INDEX

Printed in the United States
130213LV00002B/35/P